ABORTION ETHICS IN A NUTSHELL

A PRO-*BOTH* TOUR OF THE MORAL ARGUMENTS

Matt Deaton, Ph.D.

I0389515

NOTAEDPRESS

Abortion Ethics in a Nutshell:

A Pro-*Both* Tour of the Moral Arguments

By Matt Deaton, Ph.D.

Published by Notaed Press

Audiobook ISBN 978-1-951677-08-4

e-Book ISBN 978-1-951677-07-7

Hardcover ISBN 978-1-951677-05-3

Paperback ISBN 978-1-951677-06-0

Cover Art by Tracye Sowders

Editing by Eric Wyman

Proofing by Angelina Clendenin

For the reasonable
adult in us all.

Acknowledgments

Thanks to my first ethics teacher, Lin Rankin, for introducing me to the philosopher's approach to morality. In my early twenties, after a short stint in the Air Force and anticipating a career in medicine, you made what I worried would be a chore one of my favorite classes. Still is.

Thanks to Professor John Hardwig for serving as an intellectual mentor for the past fifteen years. We disagree on much. But my understanding is what it is due in large part to your insights, challenges and generous willingness to discuss.

Thanks to my ethics students at the University of Texas at Tyler for treating this issue with the respect and care it deserves. You've expanded my understanding and forgiven my flaws. Thank you for your insights and inspiration.

Thanks also to Greg Bock, Charles Cardwell, Paul Johnson, Court Lewis, John McClellan, John Pierce, Ben Sharpton and Len Zeller for your invaluable feedback and suggestions on this manuscript.

Finally, thanks to anyone accepting the challenge to reason through abortion ethics in good faith. A willingness to explore it anew is rare. Kudos for having the curiosity. And the guts.

Contents

Introduction

A Better Way

Protestors screaming, politicians scaring, pundits spreading spite. Shallow judgments, stifled progress, perpetual division and scorn.

There has to be a better way. A way that listens. A way that cares. A way of nuanced, principled balance. A way that puts truth above power. A way of compassion and respect.

This is that way—the philosopher's way. Welcome.

Can (and Should) Men Discuss Abortion?

I'll never experience what it's like to be pregnant. If you're male, neither will you. For us, procreation is as easy as it is enjoyable. It's women who suffer the burdens and dangers, the risks to life and health, the impact on their plans, commitments and very identity.

Despite this obvious fact, men sometimes barge into abortion discussions with smug condescension, willfully ignorant of how bearing a child is dangerous, disruptive and irreversibly life-changing, pretending pregnancy is like wearing a pink jacket for nine months. An understandable response has been to ask anyone lacking a womb to kindly butt out.

However, reasonable, respectful men can and should discuss abortion ethics, for we need all thoughtful hands on deck. And while the perspective of women is absolutely essential, for any issue, neither personal risk nor direct experience are necessary to contribute.

You're not the president, but know an executive abuse of power when you see one. You're (probably) not a combat vet, but understand why targeting civilians is wrong. You're not a convicted murderer, but hold some view on capital punishment. We needn't be journalists to challenge censorship, girls to object to female genital mutilation, Hell's Angels to dispute helmet laws.

Perspective often helps. I can't fully appreciate the pressures of police work, and so can only humbly judge officers' split-second mistakes. But sometimes being a disinterested third party is an advantage. A murderer on death row would have a tough time fairly assessing state executions. The same for the family of a murder victim. The same for a president worried about impeachment or a Marine facing a court-martial.

The main requirements are that we bring an open mind, a willingness to follow wherever reason leads and an agreement to cooperatively and kindly pursue the truth.

Of course, this isn't the norm. Everyone desperately wants to be right, which leads us to defend whatever we *think* we believe or what we think we're supposed to believe or what we've been taught righteous people believe. We wind up cherry-picking affirming arguments and dismissing everything else. But this isn't a fault unique to men, and it isn't a sin that you and I haven't committed. We can all do better. And earnestly trying to do better is critical, for we've inherited a caustic culture decades in the making.

Fear, Control and Transcendence

Whether you lean pro-choice or pro-life, you've probably been conditioned to believe the "other" side isn't simply stupid, but evil. "They" want to control you, to tear the social order apart or to return it to its oppressive roots. "They" aren't to be reasoned with, listened to or trusted. In some circles, "They" are simply the enemy, and enemies are better destroyed than engaged in conversation.

This is the message of pulpit bullies and demagogues, Facebook memes and viral tweets, fame-drunk influencers and millions of well-intentioned followers under their spell.

Our goal is to transcend that madness, to cut through the fog and intelligently think through the issue as mature adults. Spoiler: the traditional pro-vs-pro paradigm is a grossly oversimplified myth. Both sides are motivated by legitimate concerns. But neither holds a monopoly on moral truth. The "Rate That Abortion" exercise in Chapter 4 should leave little doubt that real cases in the real world don't fit into neat "for" or "against" boxes.

So why do so many go on pretending one side is 100% correct and the other 100% wrong? Because we're being intentionally frightened and divided. Because afraid people watch. Afraid people click. Afraid people *vote.*

Where *Not* to Look

In 2013, I did a stint with the Congressional Research Service, a nonpartisan think tank at the Library of Congress. Hoping to help representatives consider issues objectively for a change, I learned fast what D.C. veterans take for granted: people aren't on Capitol Hill to philosophize. They're there to win.

Invited to a Georgetown-hosted speaker series on how Congress works, I was excited to see a former congressman from my home state on the schedule. Even though I was a tad starstruck, I approached him beforehand and introduced myself. He seemed nice enough.

The topic of his presentation: a day in the life of a House of Representatives member. He spoke of breakfast with party leadership, review of updated talking points, confirmation of voting marching orders. I kept waiting for the bipartisan brunch, when I assumed Democrats and Republicans sat down to figure out what's truly in the best interests of the country. If not daily, surely they met weekly. Monthly? But it never came. So I raised my hand.

"Sir, when does the deliberation happen? You know,

when members from all sides get together and think through which solutions are truly best? Most just?" He paused with a smirk, shifted toward me and offered a thinly veiled insult about how leaders from my hometown had once requested his assistance. "These people were so *stupid,*" he said, turning what I thought was a fair question into a chance to embarrass a naïve newbie.

What I had to learn was that sincere deliberation, if it's to happen at all, has to happen among *us.* Elected officials see little benefit in earnest conversation. Negotiate, sure. But deliberate? What would be the point? By the time most people achieve political power, they're not open to reconsidering what justice should be. They're too busy trying to force their set vision on the rest of us.

Don't look to the media, either. Postman and Powers taught us in *How to Watch TV News* that since CNN competes with HBO and ESPN for eyeballs, we should expect the spastic fluff we get. There are exceptions. But generally, viewers are tantalized and angered, frightened and entertained—whatever it takes to keep us from flipping to Comedy Central or Netflix.

Then there's the bias. Just as Fox News has its ideological expectations, so does The New York Times. Storylines that don't fit the expected narrative are simply nixed.

In my wiser moments, I follow Cal Newport's advice

in *Digital Minimalism* and avoid the news altogether. But when I do indulge, my strategy is to flip between MSNBC and Fox, Russia TV and CNN, The New York Times and Drudge Report, in the hope that I might cobble together some semblance of the truth. If nothing else, maybe I can understand what people who only read the Times or only watch Fox are thinking. But I'm not confident a bouquet of reality can be plucked from a field of half-truths.

The moral of the story: you can't rely on anyone to tell you what to think about much of anything, including abortion. In fact, you can't even rely on me. I hold up the philosopher's approach as an ideal. But Plato himself suffered the same judgment-clouding flaws as the rest of us.

We'll survey some of the better arguments professional ethicists have offered, and I'll share a few clues on which make more or less sense. But the arguments, my summaries and commentary are all subject to the same human error.

So in all cases, absorb, reflect and trust *your* judgment. Be open. But be vigilant—actively fight our shared tendency to confirm what we want to believe. You're poised to develop a richer view on abortion than you thought possible. But it won't be a view you passively receive.

Spoilers

Chapters 1, 2 and 3 briefly cover three key questions:

"What should we call it (baby, fetus, something else)?", "Is it alive (and if so, what are the implications)?" and "Does it have a soul (aka, what role should religious reasoning play)?" Much like "Should men discuss abortion ethics?", these are best addressed early.

In Chapter 4 you'll score scenarios according to how the details impact a candidate abortion's morality. If you're honest, this will draw out the *whys* behind your initial view and highlight opportunities for revision. It will also illustrate why the pro vs. pro status quo is sorely inadequate.

Then we'll work through chapters devoted to variances that seem to make a moral difference. Rather than pushing pro-this or pro-that, I'll be arguing that abortion ethics turn on at least six factors:

I. **The Nature of the Conception**
   a. Was the sex consensual or forced? To what degree?
   b. Was conception intentional or accidental? If accidental, were precautions taken?

II. **The Mother's Interests**
   a. Her health and life
   b. Her education, career and other life plans
   c. Her very identity

III. **The Status of the Entity Growing Inside Her**[1]

---

[1] We'll decide what to call this entity in Chapter 1.

a. Never a full person, but always a potential person, possessing some (possibly substantial) value from conception
b. Increasing in value over the course of gestation, as features of personhood emerge and survival becomes more certain

IV. The Child's Quality of Life[2]

a. Biological: Likely healthy or plagued by debilitating, painful disease? How likely?
b. Circumstantial: Born into a loving family in a flourishing, supportive society, or into a neglectful system in a famine-stricken, failed state?

V. The Father's Autonomy

a. Respect for his reasonable assumptions, his investment of emotions and time, his plans and legitimate interests

VI. Impact on Third Parties

a. On siblings, grandparents and other family members who've earned consideration
b. On society at large as benefactors of future benefits or victims of future harm

If some of these seem more important than others, they are. But give each a chance. Rather than on/off, right/wrong, abortions are *more or less* morally permissible or impermissible, *more or less* justifiable or unjustifiable. Or

---

[2] Here "child" refers to the post-birth baby and adolescent.

so I'll argue. Decide for yourself whether I'm right, and if so, how much weight to assign each factor in the overall moral calculus.

Abortion *Solved?*

Then—and this is the real spoiler, so skip ahead if you prefer suspense—we'll entertain the possibility that the central tension of the abortion debate will one day be "solved" by artificial wombs. How? By allowing women to transplant rather than terminate unwanted pregnancies, simultaneously facilitating choice *and* life. As ethicists Peter Singer and Deanne Wells put it, "Abortions would in effect become early births, and the destruction of the unborn would cease," enabling sworn enemies from the decades-long abortion wars to "embrace in happy harmony."[3]

Given how abortion is near the tip of the wedge dividing us, it isn't hyperbolic to suggest resolving the debate could save our republic. However, there are reasons to temper the enthusiasm.

So we'll consider the costs, the risks, worries surrounding the influx of orphans, as well as the argument that even when we can medically end a pregnancy without ending a life, we should still allow parents to terminate unwanted offspring when they so choose. And notice that

3 "Ectogenesis," chapter two of the anthology *Ectogenesis: Artificial Womb Technology and the Future of Human Reproduction* edited by Robert Ginsberg and Peter Redpath, Rodopi, 2006, page 12.

how we decide this "right to terminate" question has implications not only for the incubator-era abortions of the future, but the late-term abortions of today.

One Warning, One Request

Last, warning that rape will be discussed. Not in vivid detail. But its mention is unavoidable—not only because so many build exceptions for rape into their views on abortion, but because the reasons motivating those exceptions are worth exploring.

Few experiences are more traumatic, and you never know whether the person sitting next to you is a victim. So if you'll be discussing this with others—and I hope you will—please do so with dignity and tact.

In fact, please discuss abortion generally with dignity and tact. Whatever arguments we consider and conclusions we entertain, the purpose is never to condescend, and certainly never to induce guilt. Our attitude is collaborative and our gaze future-oriented—not on what we used to think or may have done, but on how we can improve our understanding and make better decisions tomorrow. Please attribute any mistakes I make in that regard to clumsiness rather than malice.

Thank you for your willingness to reason through abortion in good faith. And if you'd like to discuss any of this directly, find me at MattDeaton.com.

Chapter 1
What to Call It...

Terrorist or freedom fighter? Sporting rifle or assault weapon? Inheritance tax or death tax? Word choice can shape a discussion before it even begins.

When it comes to abortion, are we talking about a warm, cuddly *baby?* Or a cold, parasitic *fetus?* The words we choose not only reveal our biases, but influence our conclusions.

In *Beyond the Abortion Wars,* Charlie Camosy offers "prenatal child."[4] "Prenatal" seems fair. But "child" suggests playground laughter and Halloween masks, ballet recitals and birthday parties.

Yet, at the other extreme, Katha Pollitt argues in *Pro: Reclaiming Abortion Rights* that "fetus" is actually too generous.

> Unfortunately, there is no politically neutral general term that accurately covers the whole nine months, at least none that sounds like an English word ("conceptus"?), but "fetus" inaccurately suggests that late abortion is the norm.[5]

---

4 William B. Eerdmans Publishing, 2015, page 10.
5 Picador, 2014, introduction, eBook location 196.

So should we call it an embryo, zygote, fetus, baby? And what are the stakes? If it's a prenatal child, is abortion automatically wrong? If it's a conceptus, is abortion automatically OK?

No and no. Labeling the Affordable Care Act "Obamacare" might make it more or less attractive depending on the audience. But the law's substance—helpful, harmful or benign—remains the same.

The UDH

For the sake of clearheaded analysis, we need accurate and neutral language. My humble suggestion: Unborn Developing Human.

1. **"Unborn"** emphasizes how it's dependent upon and encapsulated within the mother, acknowledging the fact that it impacts the mother's health and wellbeing, and that it needs her continued support to exist.
2. **"Developing"** highlights the fact that it's a work in progress, gradually becoming endowed with morally relevant features over the course of gestation. These include the ability to feel pleasure and pain, consciousness and the ability to engage in (basic) relationships. The capacity for deep cognition, essential to autonomy and full personhood, won't come until years after birth.

But the seed is there from the beginning in our DNA.[6]

3. **"Human"** simply designates the species. Were it equine or canine, there wouldn't be much fuss. But rather than a Palomino or a Pug, we're talking about an entity capable of living a life similar to yours and mine.

Not as warm as baby, but not as cold as fetus, UDH is awkward for folks from both sides of the traditional debate. Yet I've used it to facilitate calm, highbrow discussion for over a decade.

I hope you find the term fair enough, or can at least appreciate the intent behind it. But if nothing else, I bet we can agree on the acronym order, UDH being clearly better than DUH, or *duh.*

---

[6] In Chapter 7 we'll consider the view that a UDH's moral status increases during gestation as various features of personhood come online and it becomes more likely to survive into a full person. If a third trimester abortion would seem more problematic than the morning-after pill, your intuitions may align with this "gradualist" view.

Chapter 2

Is It Alive?

My daughter once brought home a worksheet called "Living or Non-Living." On the living side she had pasted pictures of a flower, a fox, a snail, a fish, a tree, some grass and kids holding hands. On the non-living side she had placed a shoe, a skateboard, a bathtub, a spoon, a toaster, a ball and a pot. Her 3rd grade teacher gave it an A+.

Is a UDH more like a fox or a shoe? A tree or a spoon? A flower or a skateboard? Reflecting on our common-sense understanding of biological life, a thing is alive when it responds to stimuli, grows and possesses the ability to (eventually) reproduce.

Prior to birth, prior to viability, prior to awareness, prior to a heartbeat, fingers or toes, the sperm hits the egg and replication of a unique DNA sequence begins. This seems the best time to acknowledge the beginning of a distinct human life.

This doesn't mean conception is when a UDH becomes a full *person*. Personhood is an important moral concept we'll unpack in a coming chapter. It also doesn't mean the UDH is instantly as valuable as you or me, though its potential to develop into a creature just like you and me does endow it with *some* value. All it means is that conception is when the UDH comes alive.

Beginnings and Survival

Sometimes implantation, when the UDH embeds in the uterine wall where it will receive nourishment and protection, is cited as a morally relevant point due to the frequency of pre-implantation miscarriages. In the five to seven days between fertilization and implantation, up to half of UDHs miscarry without the woman ever knowing. However, whether a thing is likely to continue living doesn't determine when its life began.

Consider a scene from *Star Wars Episode V: The Empire Strikes Back* (like I said, highbrow discussion). Luke Skywalker and Han Solo get stranded on the surface of ice planet Hoth. With Luke freezing and barely conscious, Han uses Luke's light saber to cut open his tauntaun (a pungent kangaroo-horse creature) and shoves him inside the freshly exposed viscera. "I know this smells bad, kid. But it'll keep you alive long enough for me to build a shelter."

Back at Base Echo, C-3PO (a.k.a. *Gold Man,* as my wife calls him) conveys R2-D2's calculation that their chances of surviving a night exposed to the elements are "seven hundred and twenty-five to one." A worried Princess Leia delays dispatching a search party until morning when temperatures will rise and conditions will be safer.

All ends well the next day when a scout makes radio

contact and Luke is revived in a vat of warm fluid. But Leia was wise to postpone rescue. Safe and secure soldiers are more valuable to the Rebel Alliance than two likely to freeze to death, especially when one is a scruffy-looking nerf herder. But while Luke and Han's survivability chances may have had bearing on whether and when to try to save them, it had no bearing on when their lives began.[7]

If you'd prefer a business example, consider how most startups fail within the first six months. As Lori Greiner of NBC's *Shark Tank* would confirm, a company's early profitability therefore influences whether it's worth additional investment. But whether a business is likely to thrive is distinct from when it was founded.

The upshot: yes, UDHs are alive, independent of their chances of surviving, and independent of the fact that tiny collections of dividing cells look nothing like full-grown people. Garage-based Microsoft looked nothing like the international giant in 1975, yet that's when the company began. A sprouting acorn looks nothing like a mighty oak, yet it's alive.

Relax

If you're worrying we just took a hard turn towards a sweeping pro-life conclusion, stop. Just because UDHs are

---

[7] We'll return to the moral significance of survival probabilities in Chapter 7: The UDH's Value.

alive doesn't mean we have an absolute obligation to keep them alive any more than Leia had an absolute obligation to rescue Luke and Han or Lori has an absolute obligation to finance every business she's pitched.

Despite what the pop culture debate suggests, there's more to abortion ethics than when life begins. Much more. But before we dive into what that might be, let's take an important detour through political philosophy and the concept of public reason.

Chapter 3

Does It Have a Soul?

If asked whether a UDH has an immortal soul, a Muslim might offer one answer, a Hindu a second and a Christian a third. A Catholic might quibble with an Episcopalian. A Shiite might disagree with a Sunni. And a Buddhist might join hands with an Agnostic and question the existence of souls altogether.

Since souls are a matter of faith, this doesn't seem a question we can answer as a group. In fact, given our vast diversity, discussing abortion ethics at all might seem impossible. How could Shaivites and Southern Baptists ever find common ground?

Well, there might be a way. What if we could transcend the divisions while keeping the wisdom? See if you can guess which group published the following:

> The topic of abortion evokes strong and varied convictions about the social order, the roles of women and men, human life and human responsibility, freedom and limits, sexual morality, and the significance of children in our lives. It involves powerful feelings that are based on different life experiences and interpretations of <*guess which religion*> faith and life in the world. If we are to take

> our differences seriously, we must learn how to talk about them in ways that do justice to our diversity. The language used in discussing abortion should ignore neither the value of unborn life nor the value of the woman and her other relationships. It should neither obscure the moral seriousness of the decision faced by the woman nor hide the moral value of the newly conceived life.

Could you tell whether it was written by Methodists or Mennonites? Atheists or Jews? All I can tell is that it's eloquent and insightful, and that it comes from a place of empathy and respect.

As it happens, it was written by Evangelical Lutherans.[8] But apart from the word "Christian," which is what the original said *<here>*, it's grounded in reasons anyone should be able to appreciate independent of their faith commitments or lack thereof. These are exactly the sorts of reasons we owe one another in the public forum.

Convincing and Respectful

If we want our arguments to be taken seriously, and if we want to show people of different backgrounds adequate respect, we can't simply cite scripture. Our

---

[8] *A Social Statement on Abortion.* "This social teaching statement was adopted by a more than two-thirds majority vote at the second biennial Churchwide Assembly of the Evangelical Lutheran Church in America, meeting in Orlando, Florida, August 28-September 4, 1991."

arguments have to appeal to anyone, not only those who happen to share our faith.

Most people intuitively understand this. The Qur'an is rarely quoted in mixed company. But if religious moral reasoning is the only moral reasoning we've known, we may be understandably reluctant to try another approach.

For one, we may worry we'll dishonor our faith or stumble toward conclusions we won't want to accept. Plus, if we're convinced our holy text expresses the inerrant word of God, it's understandable to want to share it. Rather than hiding it under a bush, why not do all we can to ensure it's not only widely known, but followed?

To see why, imagine being a woman in a Taliban-controlled region of Afghanistan. It's illegal for you to vote, read or show your face in public. Women who dare challenge their husbands are publicly flogged or even beheaded. And tribal leaders—similar to you in every way except sex organs—justify your treatment on grounds that it follows from their interpretation of Islam.

Imagine living as a Dalit "Untouchable" in India. You're excluded from all but the worst jobs, openly mocked and taught to view yourself as inherently unclean. You see Dalit men beaten and Dalit women raped with impunity. And the officials who enable your persecution—similar to you in every way except inherited caste—justify your treatment on grounds that it follows from their interpretation of Hinduism.

Or imagine living as a slave in 1800s New York. You're shackled, whipped, torn from your family and sold as property. The US Constitution counts you as three-fifths of a person for representation purposes (see Article 1, Section 2, Clause 3). And many voters, legislators and even judges—similar to you in every way except skin pigment—justify your treatment on grounds that it follows from their interpretation of Christianity.

The problem isn't that religion always spreads injustice. Not at all. The vast majority of Muslims reject the Taliban's interpretation of Islam. Devout Hindus are among the most aggressive reformers of India's caste system. And American Christians were a driving force behind slavery's abolition and the Civil Rights Movement 100 years later.

Rather, the problem is that using a religion not accepted by all to justify coercive policies disrespects nonbelievers and believers alike. It's bad enough when we disagree with a law. But it's worse when those who force it upon us know the reasons supporting it have limited rational appeal.

Required by the Golden Rule?

Christian philosopher Robert Audi argues that the Golden Rule actually requires that we resist the temptation to use the state to enforce purely religious conceptions of morality on others.[9] Why? If we found ourselves in the religious minority—perhaps a non-Muslim Afghan woman, a non-Hindu Indian Dalit, or a non-Christian American slave (or someone who accepted the faith, but not the ruling group's interpretation)—we'd want the laws governing our treatment decided with reasons that made sense to us.

If you're Christian, you'll have to decide for yourself whether Audi's argument is truly consistent with the faith. But author and world religions professor Barbara Brown Taylor explains that the Golden Rule should have wide appeal.

> "Hurt not others in ways that you yourself would find hurtful." That one is from Judaism. "None of you is a believer until you love for your brother what you love for yourself." That one is from Islam. "This is the sum of duty: do not do to others what would cause pain if done to you." That one is from Hinduism. Some version of the principle shows up in all the great religions of the world, which is a large part of what makes them great: they ask members inside the tribe to use their humanity as the benchmark for how to treat those outside the tribe.[10]

Now let's add a brief argument from philosopher

---

9 Religious Commitment and Secular Reason. Cambridge University Press, New York, 2000.
10 *Holy Envy: Finding God in the Faith of Others.* HarperOne, 2019, page 76.

Thomas Nagel supporting that same Golden Rule.

> [E]ach person has a reason to consider not only his own interests but the interests of others… to consider the effect of what he does on the good or harm of everyone… I may want to jump into an icy river to save a drowning stranger not because it will make me feel good, but because I recognize that his life is important, just as mine is, and I recognize that I have a reason to save his life just as he would have a reason to save mine if our positions were reversed.[11]

Nagel illuminates what we intuitively appreciate already—that since there's no relevant difference between ourself and the next person (sharing common capacities, drives, fears, desires), if we'd expect and want them to treat us a certain way, logical consistency demands that we treat them similarly. As Nagel puts it, "I recognize that his life is important" to him, just as my life is important to me. And given our relevant similarities, I have "reason to consider not only [my] interests but the interests of others."

Tada: the same Golden Rule, only now with a little philosophical flair.

Public Reasoning, Personal Humility

Nagel's argument is convincing not necessarily

---

[11] "Right and Wrong" from *What Does It All Mean?* Oxford University Press, 1987, pages 335 & 337.

because his conclusion aligns with our religious commitments, but because it's built on moral sentiments most of us share. Whatever our background or faith, our sense of fairness tells us we should treat like cases alike. We agree that the consequences of our actions matter. We expect people to treat one another with respect rather than as mere tools. We recognize something special about our relationships with loved ones and find it not only morally permissible, but sometimes morally required, to place their interests above our own. And we know developing good character is essential to living a good life.

These are examples of what philosophers call "public" reasons. They don't depend on a particular holy book or unique cultural norms. Rather, they're embedded in our shared experience as human beings.

Philosophers have used some of them to develop full-blown ethical theories: Utilitarianism is based on consequences, Kantianism on rationality and respect, Care Ethics on relationships and Virtue Ethics on character. If you're familiar, great. But if not, no worries. The requirement is simply that we offer and be open to reasons with rational appeal to all. Most of us do this naturally. We're just making the expectation explicit.

Relax (Again)

If you're religious, don't worry that only considering

public abortion arguments will necessarily steer us toward a quick and coarse pro-choice conclusion. In the last chapter we decided UDHs are alive without any reference to religion whatsoever. And just as that didn't push us to one extreme, setting aside scripture won't push us to the other. In fact, there are compelling public arguments both generally for and against abortion. And while no author settles all aspects decisively, each will illuminate some key piece of the puzzle.

However, know that the idea isn't that faith should play no role. Instead, it's that faith-based views need to be justifiable from a shared perspective, especially if we hope to use them to influence public policy.

If a religious understanding suggests something a nonbeliever would almost surely reject (beheading women for reading, perpetuating the Untouchables travesty, slavery), or it rests on a claim that can't be supported with public reasons (that UDHs are ensouled at conception or that childbirth must be painful), then we should set it aside. But if it suggests something that seems reasonable, put on your philosopher's hat and test whether it's truly defendable absent theological support. And not superficially defendable, as in, "Yeah, I could imagine a moron buying this..." But genuinely defendable, as in, "Yes, after careful reflection I earnestly believe an intelligent, objective person could find this public argument convincing."

However, be warned that our egos are cunning. If we

let them, they'll inflate arguments that confirm our biases, convincing us whatever we argued most recently—especially if we argued loudly—must be true. They'll discount ideas that might lead to the terrible fate of changing our minds. Plenty of arguments were offered in support of slavery. Of course, none of them were any good. Yet the fear of losing face (and power) led people to suppress the obvious, pound their fists and continue defending the indefensible.

Begin your exploration of abortion ethics from wherever you are. But if it becomes clear a position can't withstand scrutiny, have the courage to examine it anew. Barbara Brown Taylor, the author and professor who shared the Golden Rule's many religious appearances, is also an Episcopal priest. Her advice on resolving tension between our religious interpretations and our considered convictions: dig deeper.

> When I run into a hard corner of Christian thinking about the subordination of women, I remember that the angel Gabriel did not ask Mary's father if it would be all right for her to bear a son out of wedlock; Gabriel asked her. When I am walloped by Christian condescension toward those who are not Christian, I remember how many religious strangers played lead roles in Jesus's life: the Canaanite woman who expanded his sense of agency, the Samaritan leper

> who showed him what true gratitude looked like, the Roman centurion in whom he saw more faith than he had ever seen in one of his own tribe… This is one of the reasons why I remain a devoted student of the Bible: because what it says is so often *not* what I have been taught it says, or what I think it says, or what I want it to say. Scripture has its own voice—sometimes more terrible than wonderful—but it has never failed to reward my close attention, either with a fresh hearing or with the loud slamming of a door that tells me to come back later.[12]

You're welcome to handle differences between your religious and nonreligious judgments however you see fit. Some mentally segregate the two, using religious reasoning to guide personal decisions and public reasoning to deliberate with others and vote.

However, Convergence Theory is the idea that a full and proper understanding of a true holy text should point to the same conclusions as a full and proper understanding of the best nonreligious arguments. If a deity endowed us with these big brains and an innate moral sense, surely we'd be expected to use them. So why not put our best secular moral understandings in conversation with scriptural exegesis and vice versa?

And if there's anything to Audi's Golden Rule

[12] *Holy Envy*, page 105.

argument, maybe a loving, omnipotent deity would appreciate believers humble and respectful enough to try.

Maybe. But as Taylor cautions, using our imperfect human brains to infer what an infinitely intelligent being might think is a stretch. Her self-reminder: "The minute I believe I know the mind of God is the minute someone needs to sit me down and tell me to breathe into a paper bag."[13]

Of course, a religious life requires *some* insight into the mind of God. Otherwise, how would believers know how to live? Taylor is simply arguing that rigid certitude is foolhardy. And on this point, philosophers definitely agree.

Yeah, You Too

Lest there be any confusion, nonreligious folks need humility just as much as religious folks—sometimes more. When it comes to ego fragility, we all live in glass houses. None of us are above the sin of intellectual arrogance, including me.

But by reasoning together in good faith, cooperatively rather than competitively, progress is possible. I've seen it in the classroom, I've felt it myself and I'm convinced it's the only way we'll figure out abortion. Thank you for joining the conversation, and for giving the philosopher's approach a fair try.

---

[13] Ibid, page 108.

Chapter 4

Rate That Abortion

Please score the following scenarios on a scale of 0 to 5. Don't worry what you're supposed to think or what others might think—this doubles as a self-honesty test. Simply reflect and mark your best guess estimates, ideally in pencil.

If you tend to lean pro-choice, 0s are for cases where the reasons are the least compelling, even if you'd still support the pregnant woman if she chose to abort. 5s, however, are the gold standard, reserved for cases where the abortion would be unquestionably justifiable. For everything in between, use 1s, 2s, 3s, 4s and decimals if you'd like.

If you're inclined to lean pro-life, 5s are for cases when aborting would be most understandable, most forgivable, even if still ultimately wrong. 0s are for the worst of the worst—the clearest cases of an unethical, immoral abortion. Use scores in between according to the details.

The honesty required here means no self-censorship. You need to clarify what you currently believe, even if you can't fully explain why, and to get a general idea of which details seem to make a moral difference. We'll unpack the why later.

A: Amanda's pregnancy is the result of rape.[14]

B: Bianca's pregnancy is the result of rape and she is a known prostitute.

***Note:** You may be thinking, "What does her occupation have to do with it?" The answer: maybe nothing. That's for you to decide. Reflect and score accordingly.

C: Celeste's pregnancy is the result of rape, she is thirteen years old and the rapist is her mother's boyfriend.

D: Daniela's pregnancy is the result of rape and she has waited until 23 weeks gestational age to request an abortion.

***Note:** According to The American College of Obstetricians and Gynecologists, at 23 weeks a UDH would have roughly a 25% chance of surviving with Neonatal Intensive Care, though the child would likely suffer disabilities including "cerebral palsy, blindness, profound hearing loss" or significant developmental delays.[15] For UDHs born a week earlier at 22 weeks, researchers found that "death rates were 97-98% with just 1% surviving without neurodevelopmental

---

[14] This exercise was created by ethics professors at the University of Tennessee in the 1990s. Thanks to Drs. Glenn Graber, John Hardwig, Annette Mendola and others for sharing it, and for the thumbs up to include it here. I've tweaked the wording, added names and one new case. Friend and colleague, Court Lewis, and coauthor, Timothy Dick, use a similar version in *Medical Ethics: A Case Consult Approach,* Kendall Hunt, 2019.

[15] "Periviable Birth," *Obstetric Care Consensus,* No. 6, Oct 2017 published by The American College of Obstetricians and Gynecologists. https://www.acog.org/clinical/clinical-guidance/obstetric-care-consensus/articles/2017/10/periviable-birth

impairment."[16] And for UDHs born a week later at 24 weeks, "55% of neonates survived and 32% survived without evidence of neurodevelopmental impairment."[17] A UDH at 23 weeks would also have the beginnings of a nervous system, but experts disagree over whether it would be able to perceive pain. If genuine pain requires self-reflection, its cortex wouldn't be sufficiently developed until the third trimester. But if raw sensations alone count, pain could be perceivable as early as 12 weeks.[18]

E: Elaine claims that the pregnancy was the result of rape, but the father, Eddie, claims she agreed to becoming pregnant, and he wants to take the child to raise himself.

F: Faith acknowledges that she and her boyfriend, Fernando, planned the pregnancy, but she has changed her mind and wants an abortion. Fernando insists that Faith continue the pregnancy and offers to take the child to raise himself.

G: Gale is in early pregnancy and has invasive cancer of the cervix. If her uterus is removed promptly, she has a good chance of survival. The operation will result in the death of the UDH whose development would otherwise be normal.

H: Same as (G), except Hannah doesn't want an abortion, preferring to run the risk of a spread of the cancer rather

---

[16] Ibid (same source).
[17] Ibid.
[18] "Reconsidering Fetal Pain" by Derbyshire and Bockmann, *Journal of Medical Ethics* 2020; 46:3-6. Note that the authors don't argue that the possibility that early-term UDHs might sense pain is reason to stop abortions, but to take steps to make them painless.

than to kill the UDH. Her husband Henry, however, urges that she have the hysterectomy, insisting that he and their three existing children, Holly, Harry and Helio, need her to live.

I: Genetic screening of parents Ingrid and Ivan reveals that their male offspring have a 50% chance of being born with hemophilia, a condition that inhibits blood clotting and can cause joint pain, nosebleeds and increased susceptibility to bleeding into the brain. Amniocentesis shows that this UDH is male.

J: Genetic screening of parents J and Janelle reveals that their female offspring have a 25% chance of a disorder which produces severe mental handicaps. Amniocentesis shows that this UDH is female.

K: Amniocentesis at week 6 reveals that Kathy's UDH has Tay-Sachs disease, a fatal genetic condition which causes the progressive loss of senses and mobility, leading to paralysis and death in early childhood.[19]

L: Same as (K), except that the lab mistakenly delayed release of Latoya's amniocentesis results until 23 weeks gestational age.

***Note:** It's easy to fall into a binary trap. If you're scoring these all 0s or all 5s, please take a break and start over. Shooting deer for sport is justifiable. Shooting deer for food

---

[19] For more on Tay-Sachs, visit the Cameron and Hayden Lord Foundation at lordfoundation.org.

is more justifiable. Stealing an apple from a grocery store is wrong. Stealing a homeless man's only apple is more wrong. Abortions are similarly more or less justifiable, more or less wrong. Also, if a scenario isn't providing as many details as you'd like, invent some, make a note, and score. "Assuming *this*, I'd score it a 3. If instead assuming *that*, I'd score it a 4."

M: A baby would place a severe financial strain on parents Michael and Michaela who already have four children, Miranda, Melanie, Matthew and Martin. In spite of Michael working two jobs and Michaela taking work when she can, they are barely able to afford food, housing and clothing.

N: Nadia is in early pregnancy and is suffering from chronic hypertensive heart disease associated with severe renal insufficiency. If she continues to gestate, she may die from the increased demands on her heart and kidneys. Although aborting would kill the UDH, its chances for survival are already slight given Nadia's health problems.

O: Ophelia became pregnant due to contraceptive failure.

P: Petra became pregnant due to contraceptive failure, plus having a baby at this time would seriously jeopardize her career goals.

Q: Having a baby at this time would seriously jeopardize Quinn's career goals, but she and father Quantrill did not use any form of contraception.

R: Parents Roberta and Roberto hadn't used contraceptives because they had been told Roberta was infertile.

S: Sarah's pregnancy is the result of an extra-marital affair. Husband Saleem insists on an abortion as a condition of remaining married.

T: Tasha's pregnancy is the result of an extra-marital affair. Husband Tobias has (somewhat reluctantly) agreed to keep the child, but Tasha believes the child would be a constant cause of marital disharmony, so is requesting an abortion to preserve the marriage.

U: Ursula's husband, Urijah, left her before she learned that she is pregnant. Ursula states (and her psychiatrist agrees) that she cannot cope with a pregnancy right now.

V: Velma left her husband, Vinnie, and instituted divorce proceedings before she learned that she is pregnant. She stated, "I'll be damned if I give Vinnie the satisfaction of becoming a father!"

***Note:** Are you starting to get a feel for which details seem to make a moral difference, even if you can't articulate why? Good. We'll organize and think them through soon.

W: Wynona has serious health problems such that continuing the pregnancy would probably leave her in chronic poor health for the rest of her life, although it would not shorten her life expectancy.

X: Xena is in prolonged obstructed labor. For various reasons, a Cesarean section is not an option, and she will die unless a craniotomy (a procedure in which the UDH's head is crushed) is performed. If a craniotomy is not performed and Xena dies from uterine rupture or exhaustion, the UDH would likely die also.

Y: The pregnancy is normal, but parents Yasmine and Yasir are in a country where population is strictly controlled. If they allow the pregnancy to continue, they will suffer widespread social disapproval and economic sanctions.

Z: Amniocentesis reveals that the UDH is female, but parents Zelda and Zack want their firstborn to be male.

***Note:** Hang in there—only ten more.

AA: Amniocentesis reveals that the UDH is male, and parents Arsheen and Aaron stand to lose a large inheritance unless their firstborn is female.

BB: Just before she learned that she is pregnant, Barbara left her husband, Brad, quit her job and made a career move which she had been planning for several years. Continuing the pregnancy would disrupt that plan, which might derail her career aspirations irreversibly.

CC: Constance has a pre-viable pregnancy developing in one of her fallopian tubes instead of her uterus (an ectopic pregnancy). If an operation is not performed to excise the UDH or remove the tube containing it, she may die from a spontaneous tubal rupture. Although the operation would kill the UDH, it is extremely unlikely it could in any case survive.

DD: Just before Dacia learned that she is pregnant, she made reservations for a long-dreamed-of trip around the world. If she continues the pregnancy, she will miss out on the trip and lose a substantial deposit.

EE: Same as (DD), except Eva will be accompanied by her mother, Esther, who is dying of cancer and whose last wish is to take this trip with Eva.

FF: Same as (DD), except Florencia is inclined to cancel the trip and gestate. However, her husband, Fabio, wants her to abort and take the trip to minimize the impact on their finances.

GG: Gabby is a heroin addict and unlikely to agree to rehabilitation if the pregnancy continues.

HH: Father Hank is a heroin addict and unlikely to agree to rehabilitation if the pregnancy continues, though he promises to do so if mother Hanita aborts.

II. No contraception was used because neither young Isabelle nor her boyfriend Ignacio planned to "go all the way." Having a baby now would seriously disrupt Isabelle's plans for finishing college and beginning her chosen career.

JJ: Same as (II), except young Janet has had two previous abortions for the same reason.

Initial Analysis

Which scenarios did you find toughest to score? Easiest? Which were the most enlightening? Most awkward?

You may have noticed that certain details seemed to

make a moral difference. These might have included the nature of the conception (consensual, forced, intentional or accidental), the pregnancy's impact on the mother (to her health, her life, her relationships and plans), the UDH's stage of development (early, late, somewhere between), the resulting child's likely quality of life (their health, family situation, general prospects for happiness), the desires of the father and even impacts on third parties. We'll explore how much weight to assign each of these in later chapters.

However, your thinking is likely evolving already. Before a bioethics professor gave this exercise to me, I'd never considered half of these scenarios. Abortion suddenly became complex, and the old pro-choice vs. pro-life paradigm strikingly inadequate. Coarse slogans work great on protest signs. But for real cases in the real world, not so much.

Briefly revisit the situations that gave you the most pause. If you're reluctant to change your scores, know that revising for good reason is a mark of maturity, not weakness. Question the motives of anyone who tells you otherwise. My own scores aren't set in stone. Because however much I think I know, I can always learn more.

Chapter 5

The Nature of the Conception

Imagine waking tomorrow to find a stranger sleeping beside you. Drowsy and confused, you feel a tightness in your arm and discover medical tubes leeching blood from your body into the stranger's. He's sickly pale and clutching sheet music for some reason. Just as you reach to rip the needle from your arm, a man in a tuxedo steps out of your closet.

> "Good morning! I'm Jason with The Society for Music Lovers. The gentleman to your left is a famous violinist—one of the world's *greatest* violinists, in fact. He's contracted a terrible disease which will kill him without your help. We've studied your medical records (your family doctor is a member of The Society) and you possess very rare blood—the *only* blood that can save his life. The good news is that you only have to remain connected to him for a few months. We apologize for the inconvenience and do hope you understand."

Were you to find yourself in this situation, do you think you would have a moral obligation to stay connected, or would it be OK to disconnect and walk (or run) away? It's sad that the violinist will die without your help. But you didn't volunteer to be his blood donor. You went to bed per usual, and this "Society" hijacked your body. Remaining connected would be kind for sure. But since you didn't consent to any of this, it would seem you have little obligation to help.

Ethicist Judith Jarvis Thomson used this now-famous scenario to argue that having a violinist forced upon you by The Society for Music Lovers is similar to having a pregnancy forced upon you by a rapist.[20] In both cases, an innocent's life depends on the use of your body. And in both cases, you neither consented to the connection nor engaged in any activity that might have predictably led to it. Given these core similarities, if you agree that it would be OK to disconnect from the violinist, you should also agree that it's OK to abort if raped.

Jarvis Thomson's argument illuminates a link between choice and responsibility. If you don't choose to connect to the violinist, or even do something that might lead to connecting, like entering your name in a blood donor raffle, then you have no obligation to remain connected. If you don't choose to become pregnant, or even do something that might lead to pregnancy, like voluntarily having sex, then you have no obligation to gestate. If we don't choose

---

[20] "A Defense of Abortion," *Philosophy and Public Affairs*, Vol. 1, No. 1 (1971), pages 47-66. Note that Jarvis Thomson didn't use the violinist argument to explicitly defend abortion in cases of rape, but many agree it does that philosophical work nonetheless.

the act, we have no obligation to bear the consequence.

The Sliding Scale of Choice

However, choosing isn't a binary activity. Consider car sales. The ideal scenario might involve the rational, informed purchase of a quality automobile with a strong warranty. Customers would have many cars to choose from, access to specs and reviews and be under no pressure to buy. At the other end of the spectrum, the mob forces rusty clunkers on timid victims desperate for transportation, threatening to break their kneecaps if they don't make outrageous payments. In between, slick sales associates unload lemons on gullible first-time buyers.

All else equal, it would seem informed, uncoerced buyers would have the most responsibility to make their payments, mob victims would have the least, and those suckered into buying lemons more or less responsibility depending on just how manipulative their salesperson had been. The underlying principle: we're more responsible for the consequences of free and informed choices.

When this concept is applied to reproductive ethics, at one end of the spectrum we might put planned, intentional procreation by committed, competent adults. At the other end, rape. In between, teenagers succumbing to the judgment-clouding combination of hormones and their first Budweiser.

Would intentional procreation obligate a mother to gestate, similar to how an informed, rational car sale obligates a buyer to make the payments? Would voluntary but buzzed teenage sex only moderately obligate a girl to gestate, similar to how the manipulative sale of a clunker would only moderately obligate a buyer to pay?

Before deciding, let's add cases where couples choose to have sex, but don't intend to conceive. In Rate That Abortion Case P, Petra's pregnancy is the result of contraceptive failure. In Case Q, Quinn and Quantrill didn't use contraception at all. In both, having a baby would jeopardize the woman's career goals.

We're not yet in a good position to decide how career goals stack up against the value of a UDH. But the variable we're testing here is how the use of contraceptives might impact responsibility to gestate. For help, enter another creative argument by analogy from Judith Jarvis Thomson.

People Seeds?

Imagine a world in which carpet contained people seeds. People seed carpet is just like regular carpet, except when it comes in contact with pollen, a UDH is conceived. Nightmarish, I know.

Hardwood, tile, linoleum, and other alternatives are too pricey, so you install a modest gray carpet throughout your home. Humans gestating in your hallway would be a nuisance, so you install fine screens on your windows and storm doors. You invest in a pollen-destroying heating and air unit. And when the pollen count is high, you cut off your air conditioning to decrease air circulation, seal all entries and forbid nonessential traffic.

Your neighbor Bud, whose beige shag carpet is stained brown, is less cautious. Anytime it's nice out, his screenless windows are wide open. This is unfortunate because Bud also enjoys gaudy rock music. His favorite band is Jackyl, and after living next to him for five years, you know the lyrics to "Lumberjack" by heart.

One pleasant fall evening, you decide to open your bedroom window for a mere thirty minutes. Thanks to the latest pandemic, you've become desperate for fresh air and reason that enjoying nature in this limited way is essential to living a full human life. You ensure your window's pollen screen is in good working order, and even run a new pollen/virus decontaminator afterwards to cleanse your air. However, one resilient speck survives, floats into your den and promptly impregnates your carpet.

Bud's carpet is impregnated the same evening, though via a less challenging conquest. During his nightly beer binge and rock concert, Bud passes out in his doorway, allowing even more pollen to waft in than usual. Several bits land and one successfully impregnates his foyer.

Given your caution and Bud's recklessness, doesn't it

seem Bud is more responsible for his carpet's pregnancy? And in light of that disparity in culpability, doesn't Bud have more of an obligation to care for his UDH than you do for yours? After all, you made it clear through your preventative actions that you have no interest in becoming a parent right now. Wouldn't the comparative sacrifices you made partially absolve you from responsibility?

Jarvis Thomson thinks so and argues that the implication is that people who take steps to prevent pregnancy have a lessened obligation to gestate. If a couple uses birth control and the woman gets pregnant regardless, aborting would be less problematic for them than for a couple who didn't use protection.

Does this argument work? I'm not sure. Bud put his carpet at greater risk. But now that your floors are pregnant, the most relevant fact seems to be that your floors are pregnant. You handled yourself more maturely. But you did succumb to the temptation of fresh air, choosing to put your carpet at risk. Do your and Bud's actions pre-conception influence your responsibility to nurture an unwanted UDH post-conception?

Sex and Responsibility

Ethicist Margaret Olivia Little says no. She argues that while unprotected, casual sex may be morally objectionable, this has no bearing on whether a pregnant woman has an obligation to bring a UDH to term.

> Even if the norms [of sexual morality] are broached—one has sex in callous disregard to its potential to lead to new human life—that doesn't itself imply that one now (as punishment?) must gestate: it says one shouldn't have had that sort of sex... [T]hat one had irresponsible sex is no reason at all to bring a new person into the world.[21]

While irresponsible sex may be condemnable in light of the gravity of potential procreation, Little argues that our assessment of whether there's an obligation to gestate should focus on other factors. These might include the value of the UDH, the pregnancy's impact on the mother and the potential child's quality of life.

However, even if using birth control wouldn't influence an obligation to gestate, choosing to have sex would. Finnish bioethicist Joona Rasanen, citing Rivka Weinberg, describes the connection like this:

> [W]hen a man and woman are having sex, they implicitly accept the possible consequences of their activity. As Rivka Weinberg states, "If we do things that put our gametes at risk of joining with others and growing into persons, we assume the costs (and

---

21 "The Moral Permissibility of Abortion," *Ethics in Practice, 3rd Edition*, edited by Hugh LaFollette, Blackwell, 2007, page 155.

rewards) of that risky activity."[22]

The underlying principle: when we can reasonably predict that an activity may lead to an outcome, we bear some responsibility for the outcome if it materializes, independent of whether we took precautions to prevent it.

If I chainsaw a tree near my property line and it falls west instead of east, smashing my neighbor's fence, I now have an obligation to fix it. Regardless of whether I researched proper cutting methods, practiced on saplings, tied ropes and pulleys to the tree or wildly slung the saw around like Leatherface (while blaring Jackyl's Lumberjack), I'd still have an obligation to repair the damage. Since I'd rather avoid fence work, it's in my interest to be careful. But if I damage my neighbor's fence, my duty to repair it seems equally forceful regardless.

Perhaps the only thing that changes when I'm careful is whether and to what extent I'm *blameworthy*. If I've taken precautions, I'm more shielded from criticism. But either way, I still owe my neighbor a new fence.

Similarly, Little is arguing that while sexual recklessness is worthy of scorn, any obligation to gestate (however strong or light it may be—that's still to be determined) remains unaffected. It's the voluntariness of the choice that's paramount.

---

[22] "Ectogenesis, Abortion and a Right to the Death of the Fetus," *Bioethics*. 2017, page 701.

Case R

There's an interesting twist in Case R, in which Roberta and Roberto didn't use contraceptives because they had been told that Roberta was infertile.

With the people seeds, when you open your window for thirty minutes, you may double-check your pollen screens, make sure your AC unit is off to decrease circulation and even run your new pollen/virus-killing machine. But you know impregnated carpet remains a risk. When I cut down a tree near my neighbor's fence, I may consult with tree-cutting experts, gauge the wind and even rig up special pulleys. But I know smashing that fence remains a risk. And when a couple has sex, they may use birth control pills, condoms, spermicides and other preventative measures. But they know conception remains a risk.

However, with Case R, it's reasonable for Roberta and Roberto to believe that conceiving *isn't* a risk. If their infertility diagnosis was from a tarot card reader, they should have known better. Plus, everyone knows lab results sometimes get mixed up and doctors sometimes make mistakes. But if their source was a credible fertility specialist, and if experience confirmed the diagnosis was indeed correct, that would seem to be enough evidence to assume natural conception was impossible.

What are the implications for reproductive ethics? This is one scenario I'll leave for you to decide. How ever you think it through, reflect on the impact on abortion generally. Do your thoughts on this unique case change the way we should think about reasonable assumptions, prevention and responsibility? Is there a moral principle we should generalize and test against relevantly similar cases?

Whatever your thoughts, notice how much more there is to decide. Considering my neighbor's fence, maybe I'd have an obligation to fix it myself, pay him to fix it, hire a fencing contractor, help him round up escaping cattle, bake him a cake, all of the above or something else entirely. Voluntarily engaging in an act that we know can lead to an outcome and does, accidentally or not, seems to saddle us with a responsibility to do *something.* But what that something *is* is unclear.

The Violinist Revisited

In a world where "feminist" usually means pro-choice, bioethicist Sidney Callahan has been a vocal exception.[23] Callahan argues that the feminist values of empathy, caring and equality are actually more consistent with a pro-life approach. How?

Men have been slow to grant women equal legal rights, equal pay for equal work and equal respect. Feminists lament their marginalization and exploitation rooted in women's disproportionate procreation burden.

---

23 "A Case for Pro-Life Feminism," Commonweal 113(8), April, 1986.

When a man impregnates a woman, he can support her, but he can also disappear, leaving her with the medical risks, emotional stress and life disruption. Apart from possible court-ordered child support payments, he's free to carry on as he pleases, while she's forced to make life-changing decisions.

Feminists have traditionally argued in favor of wide access to abortion as a way to mitigate this unfairness. Just as a man can walk away from an unwanted pregnancy, abortion allows a woman to do the same.

However, Callahan argues that it's hypocritical for women to demand equal respect from men and then deny it to UDHs. If feminism is nothing more than power politics—a way for one group to enforce their preferences on others—then no big deal. But if it aspires to be a rationally defendable morality, feminists should practice what they preach. Women rightly demand equal consideration from men. They should grant the same to UDHs. As Callahan puts it:

> It is a chilling inconsistency to see pro-choice feminists demanding continued access to assembly-line, technological methods of [UDH] killing—the vacuum aspirator, prostaglandins, and dilation and evacuation. It is a betrayal of feminism, which has built the struggle for justice on the bedrock of women's empathy. After all, "maternal thinking" receives its name from a mother's unconditional

> acceptance and nurture of dependent, immature life. It is difficult to develop concern for women, children, the poor and the disposed—and to care about peace—and at the same time ignore [UDH] life.[24]

Perhaps the most controversial aspect of Callahan's argument is that she insists women should gestate when raped. Unwanted and the product of a grave sin, Callahan argues that the UDH's extreme vulnerability creates a unique opportunity to help the weak. While denying care to an entity violently forced upon us would be understandable, she argues that empathy and respect are what UDHs are owed, for it's empathy and respect that women rightly demand from men.

Notice how Callahan bases the obligation to gestate on key similarities. Both the mother and the UDH are (or at least have been) vulnerable. Both are (or at least have been) at the mercy of others. And so if one deserves compassion, argues Callahan, so does the other.

However, Jarvis Thomson's violinist argument shows why the unchosen nature of rape overrides most everything else. Unless we're willing to subject ourselves to blood conscription ambushes, we can't demand women gestate when raped. Gestating a UDH brought into existence under the worst circumstances, but through no fault of its own, would indeed be compassionate and kind. But

---

24 "A Case for Pro-Life Feminism," page 119.

requiring a woman relive that trauma daily for nine months, to sacrifice her body, to disrupt her life and relationships, would conflict with our intuitions concerning what can and can't be done to us without our permission.

I once shared the violinist analogy with a pastor friend on our way to hike Mount LeConte in the Great Smoky Mountains. He listened carefully as I asked him to imagine The Society for Music Lovers hijacking his blood supply in the night.

He paused for a few moments to reflect, then surprisingly said he wouldn't disconnect. He wouldn't welcome the inconvenience. But presumably in deference to the Golden Rule and Jesus's commandment that we love our neighbors as we love ourselves, he said he was willing to put up with the burden so the violinist could live.

Whether Christianity would truly require this, I'll leave for you to decide. But based on our everyday, common-sense morality, it doesn't seem reasonable to demand that anyone tolerate bodily abuses of this sort. If a person *volunteered* to remain connected, we might admire their generous sacrifice. But it's not something we could criticize if refused.

Chapter 6
The Mother's Interests

A right to control one's body head-to-head with a right to life ends in stalemate. Equally compelling, if one relents, the other threatens to consume it. The result: adults shaking hurtful signs, pretending the louder they yell, the more correct they become.

Part of the problem is the language of rights. Rights suggest one dominant reason overrides all others. Rights suggest discussion-ending absolutes. Rights suggest all we have to do is acknowledge the supremacy of one favored reason.

But that's not how morality works. The problem isn't that people are failing to see the overwhelming force of one powerful reason. It's that there's more than one powerful reason in play. The language of rights can't handle this and leads to a barren dead end. A superior alternative: the language of *interests.*

Some have a deep interest in becoming a parent. But pregnancy can also conflict with and destroy cherished interests. Much depends on how a particular pregnancy aligns or collides with a person's goals, commitments and identity. However, some interests are universal, including our shared interest in living a long, healthy life.

Risks to Health and Life

We've seen enough movies to know pregnancy's no big deal. You get that special glow, put up with strangers asking about your belly bump for a few months, and before you know it, everything's back to normal, right?

For some, this is apparently true. Dr. Sabrina D. MisirHiralall recently shared how her first pregnancy had been such a joy, including delivery.

> Contemplative educators often say that you can meditate through anything. Here was my chance to find out. I placed intention on developing and maintaining a peaceful, spiritual mindset during my pregnancy journey. I composed a long playlist with soft, Hindu chants. I selected music by Krishna Das and his peers because Krishna Das is a Western Hindu who blends Western and Eastern music. The religious, spiritual music created a serene aura. Since I delivered at a Catholic hospital, there was a huge wooden cross with Jesus on the wall. The lights were dim. Moonlight peered through the window. My baby was born as the sun was rising. It was the most beautiful, spiritual, experience of my life.[25]

Sabrina knows this isn't the norm. But some women truly can carry on an active lifestyle, continuing to exercise,

---

25 Email correspondence October, 2020, published with Sabrina's permission.

work and do most of the things they did pre-pregnancy. Images of fit moms-to-be twisting into warrior yoga poses come to mind. For many, though, pregnancy can be a harrowing disruption precluding all semblance of normalcy.

For example, "morning" sickness can linger and worsen the entire day, bringing wave after wave of disorienting gagging. Little shared how her sister's morning sickness involved "gut-wrenching dry heaves every 20 minutes and three hospitalizations… the equal of many an experience of chemotherapy."[26]

There's bedrest. Ordered by doctors to protect both the pregnant woman and UDH, being bedridden may sound like a welcome break. But as my wife, Lisa, explains it, "It's one thing to lie down when you want. It's another to *have* to lie down, and to only be able to get up for showers and bathroom breaks."[27]

Most of her bedrest came while pregnant with our second child to mitigate a small placental hemorrhage. Complicating matters was the fact that our three-year-old couldn't understand why Mommy wouldn't hold him. She wanted to show him her love and he wanted to receive it. But lifting him put her at risk of miscarriage, and the blood-thinning injections she self-administered twice daily meant

---

[26] "Abortion, Intimacy, and the Duty to Gestate," *Ethical Theory and Moral Practice*. Vol 2, No. 3, Ethics: Meta, Normative and Applied (Sep., 1999), page 300.
[27] Interview February, 2020, published with Lisa's permission.

complications could cause her to bleed to death. Compromised and with little to do but worry, the mental stress at times felt overwhelming.

The injections were to address a clotting issue doctors hadn't diagnosed until her second miscarriage. With her first, I had foolishly tried to console her by (what I now realize was) mansplaining that so early in the pregnancy, it wouldn't have been conscious and couldn't have felt any pain. But having already envisioned and bonded with her birthed baby to-be, my clumsy attempt at compassion was interpreted as insulting. We worked through it. But, aspiring fathers, don't repeat my mistake. Downplaying the status of the UDH is unlikely to help. Try simply holding her.

Then there's delivery. Sabrina's was the ideal. But according to the CDC, "about 700 women die each year in the United States as a result of pregnancy or delivery complications."[28] Globally it's getting better, but still terribly dangerous. According to the World Health Organization, pregnancy-related deaths decreased from over half a million in 1990 to over 300,000 in 2015.[29] The causes ranged from hemorrhage to heart conditions to infection.

Independent of the survival odds, you only have to

---

[28]https://www.cdc.gov/reproductivehealth/maternalinfanthealth/pregnancy-relatedmortality.htm

[29] "How Many Women Die in Childbirth?" by Hannah Ritchie, September 16, 2019 for *Our World in Data*. https://ourworldindata.org/how-many-women-die-in-childbirth

witness delivery once to forever respect all mothers. Lisa's first took twelve hours. Toward the end she was passing out between contractions. All I could do was pray and coach. "Wake up, Sweetie—we need you to push again." That was my modest contribution—cheerleading, plus cutting the umbilical cord while newborn Justin reached to grasp one of my fingers with his slimy little hand.

With her second, she started showing signs of preeclampsia, a life-threatening condition where blood toxins overwhelm your organs. Two weeks from the due date, our doctor decided we should induce. Rather than head-first, our daughter Emily was sitting upright, which meant a C-section was required. If I wanted to be in the room, I had to don full doctor garb: medical gown, booties, cap and mask.

I suited up and waited in the hall while the doctors initiated a spinal block. What was supposed to take five minutes stretched into ten, then fifteen. When an anesthesiologist finally came to get me, he was visibly frazzled. "The spinal didn't go perfectly so I want to prepare you before you see your wife." "Is she OK?" "She may be a little out of it."

Lisa was drowsy, barely conscious. Apparently the doctor injected too much saline, resulting in a "high spinal." We didn't know at the time, but it could have killed her. The goal was to numb her from the waist down, but the extra fluid knocked her out and wreaked havoc on her vitals.

The doctors didn't share too many incriminating details. All I can say is that they looked scared and guilty, and doctors usually don't look scared or guilty unless something has gone terribly wrong.

The procedure was otherwise successful. I got to witness live surgery and hear sweet Emily's first cries. Delivery of our third and final child, Noah, was routine.

We were fortunate. But pregnancies go sideways every day, causing harms usually overshadowed by the celebration of new life. Everyone focuses on the baby's gender and weight. Nobody wants to hear how debilitating the pregnancy was or how Mom almost died. Consider a few scenarios, all based on real life, from Rate That Abortion:

> **N:** Nadia is in early pregnancy and is suffering from chronic hypertensive heart disease associated with severe renal insufficiency. If she continues to gestate, she may die from the increased demands on her heart and kidneys.
>
> **X:** Xena is in prolonged obstructed labor. For various reasons, a Cesarean section is not an option, and she will die unless a craniotomy (a procedure in which the UDH's head is crushed) is performed.
>
> **CC:** Constance has a pre-viable pregnancy developing in one of her fallopian tubes instead of her uterus, which will kill her unless removed.

Tracye was twenty-four with her first pregnancy. She dreamed of the fun she'd have with the twin boys growing inside her. Justin and Christian would be best friends. They'd go to school together, camp together, win football games together. They'd grow up strong and bright, marry and begin beautiful families of their own.

Then, at eight months, something didn't feel right. Doctors confirmed her worst nightmare. Both had died, likely due to an undiagnosed clotting disorder.

This left Tracye and her husband devastated. While the death of their twins was tough to bear, they were determined to become parents. After some time had passed, they tried again and were cautiously thrilled to conceive. Then at home during the fourth month, she felt a pain.

> I felt slight cramping, and I knew in my heart that was wrong. I had already lost two children, so I went to the Emergency Room. I had no clue it was ectopic. Apparently, the baby had formed at the end of a fallopian tube.
>
> It ruptured in the room. It was more pain than I can describe. I fell to the floor and crawled into the hall to get the doctors' attention.
>
> I was in surgery for seven-and-a half-hours. They had to put all my blood vessels back together.
>
> During the procedure, I woke up—had what they call "anesthesia awareness." I could see the

> anesthesiologist beside me but couldn't move. I could feel what they were doing down there, but I couldn't say anything. Finally, he saw my eyes and mouthed the words, "Oh [shoot]…" The last thing I remember is more pain than I could endure.
>
> When I woke up, my husband was beside me with his head in his hands. I had died. They had to use the paddles on me three times. I don't have any memory of it—no near-death experience or anything like that. But I died three times.
>
> They hadn't caught that it was an ectopic pregnancy. The initial pain was not very significant. It was only because I had had previous [UDHs] die that I went in. If I had been at home, I would have died. And regardless of whether the mother dies [when it's ectopic], the [UDH] will certainly die.

Tracye is my second cousin. Yet I'd never heard any of this. She and her husband raised three beautiful children, and from a distance, all I saw was a joyful mother. But she volunteered her story when I invited her to design the cover for this book.[30] She's a talented artist, no?

Ectopic pregnancies are rare, but gravely dangerous. A UDH cannot gestate full term in a fallopian tube, even near the end of a tube as in Tracye's case. And when it inevitably grows large enough to cause a rupture, the

---

[30] Shared August, 2020, and published with Tracye's permission.

mother will bleed to death without emergency intervention.

Some sweeping pro-life positions deny any exceptions, maintaining that no circumstances could ever justify abortion. But when your life's in jeopardy, can't it be a legitimate act of self-preservation?

The Expanding Baby

Imagine buying a one-room cabin in the mountains. From the online ad it's small and basic, and pictures of the inside are suspiciously missing. But it's in such a beautiful spot and at such an amazing price, you can't resist.

You pack your things and arrange for your first visit. The property is as picturesque as advertised. Eager to see the interior, you ascend the porch steps and crack open the front door. The cabin is mostly bare, but in the center of the room is a wooden crib. Inside you're astonished to find a baby.

As you study it in puzzlement, you notice that it's getting bigger. It slowly doubles, then triples in size. Its body presses against and then bursts through the crib. Like an inflating Thanksgiving Day Parade balloon, it keeps getting bigger and bigger.

Puzzlement turns to panic as its expansion accelerates. You backpedal to the door and find it jammed. You try a window—no luck. The expanding baby pushes you against a wall. You scramble into a corner. If this continues, you'll soon smother or be crushed. Frantic, you remember your trusty pocketknife. But before deploying it, you pause.

The baby shows no signs of malice—it doesn't seem to be *choosing* to expand. It's not *trying* to kill you. Nevertheless, if you don't do something, it *will* kill you.

Struggling to breathe, you open the knife and jab over your shoulder, hoping to buy some time. But the prick rips into a gash, and the once expanding baby deflates into a motionless mass. With mixed emotions, you're finally able to catch your breath.

Remember Jarvis Thomson's parasitic violinist? Just as the violinist illustrated how abortion is justifiable in cases of rape, her expanding baby scenario is intended to illustrate how abortion is justifiable in cases of self-defense.[31] She argues that if you agree it would be OK to deflate the expanding cabin baby to save your life, you should also agree that it would be OK for a pregnant woman to abort a UDH to save her life.

There are, of course, differences between fictional expanding babies and real UDHs. But the key details match. It's your cabin, your body, your life. Neither the balloon baby nor the UDH act with malice. And so if your moral intuition is that it would be permissible to exercise self-defense in the first case, Jarvis Thomson argues that you should endorse it in the second.

---

31 "A Defense of Abortion," 1971.

The ethics become trickier when the threat isn't as immediate or direct. Consider Case G where "Gale is in early pregnancy and has invasive cancer of the cervix." Here it's the cancer, not the UDH, posing the threat. However, the pregnancy is delaying treatment. Gale either has to wait until delivery to begin chemo, begin chemo while pregnant and risk birth defects and miscarriage or abort to begin chemo free from the strain of pregnancy.

In reality, doctors would be able to offer recovery statistics—"You'd have *this* prognosis if we began chemo now, *that* prognosis if we began later"—which should inform the decision-making. But here we're simply acknowledging that deciding an abortion-as-self-defense case where the threat is less immediate wouldn't be as straightforward as a tubal pregnancy.

Long-Term and Mental Health

Cases where a mother's long-term health is at stake can be equally tricky. Consider Case W. "Wynona has serious health problems such that continuing the pregnancy would probably leave her in chronic poor health for the rest of her life." We'd want to know whether this chronic poor health would involve pain, and if so, how much and how frequent. We'd want to know her likelihood of developing chronic disabilities and the impact of those disabilities on her lifestyle and identity.

For example, if hiking is the principal activity that brings Wynona joy, and continuing the pregnancy would prevent her from ever hiking again, this is relevant. It would matter even more if hiking weren't simply a source of enjoyment, but central to what makes her *her*. Of course, the UDH's general moral status, its stage of development, the nature of the conception and other factors would also matter. But it's important whether she would be able to continue doing the things she loves, as well as the things central to her identity.

Consider also cases where the pregnant woman's mental health is at risk. In Case U, "Ursula's husband Urijah left her before she learned that she is pregnant. Ursula states (and her psychiatrist agrees) that she cannot cope with a pregnancy right now." Does being unable to cope mean she'd be unable to function? That she'd suffer an unrecoverable breakdown? That she might attempt suicide?

Specifics would help. But aside from the more common postpartum depression, pregnancy itself can be psychologically devastating. As Little reflected:

> I think of a friend I visited who'd been put in lock-down on the psychiatric ward from pregnancy-related psychosis (and whose physician wouldn't discuss inducing at 39 weeks because there was no "obstetrical indication").[32]

---

[32] "The Moral Permissibility of Abortion," page 152.

Education, Career and Other Life Goals

Pregnancy can also impact a woman's broader life goals. Imagine trying to sit through a college lecture or write a paper while dry heaving. Or lugging books around campus with a heavier-by-the-day UDH inside you. Even if your classes were all online, ask any mother about "mommy brain"—a drowsy, hormone imbalanced state incompatible with concentrated study.

Imagine the impact it might have at work, as in Case BB.

> Just before she learned that she is pregnant, Barbara left her husband, Brad, quit her job and made a career move which she had been planning for several years. Continuing the pregnancy would disrupt that plan, which might derail her career aspirations irreversibly.

Even if you're able to power through the mental fog, making a career move or vying for a promotion having just come off bedrest, likely to go on maternity leave soon, wouldn't be easy. Laws forbid employers from openly discriminating against pregnant women. But they can get around this in many states by keeping their reasoning private. Whether pregnancy is the official rationale, few employers prefer employees who miss work and who are drained when they're there.

If nothing else, a block of missed work could shake

an unenlightened boss's confidence in your stamina, or simply cause corrosive self-doubts. Plenty of women work through pregnancy. But gestating definitely makes things tougher, and some missed opportunities are unrecoverable.

Fundamental Identity Changes

Little argues that one of the most significant impacts of pregnancy is that bearing a child fundamentally and irreversibly changes a woman's identity. We've already considered how health risks can threaten a woman's ability to continue doing the things that make her *her.* But even when she's expected to recover physically, gestation is an intimate experience that causes an unavoidable shift in priorities and personality. Some women welcome this change. But others find themselves pregnant with no interest in such a metamorphosis—at least, not at that time. As Little explains:

> To be pregnant is to allow another living creature to live in and off one's body for nine months. It's to have one's every physical system shaped by its needs, rather than one's own. It is to share one's body in an extraordinarily intimate and extensive – and often radically unpredictable – way. Then there is the aftermath of the nine months; for gestation doesn't just turn cells into a person; it turns the woman into a mother. [A woman may not want to become a

> mother...] Not because motherhood would bring with it [terrible] burdens – though it can – but because motherhood would so thoroughly change what we might call one's fundamental identity.[33]

Ask a mother you trust how carrying a UDH changed her. Did she become less carefree? More worrisome? Did her priorities suddenly shift, whether she wanted them to or not?

Ask gently. A mother might worry her answers could suggest she doesn't love her children. Reassure her that this isn't the case at all. We can admit relationships have affected us in ways we didn't initially welcome, yet still value the relationships and persons themselves.[34]

Whatever the case, reflect on whether someone (perhaps you) might want to prevent or delay such changes, and how this and the other risks, burdens and impacts of pregnancy on a mother's varied interests should weigh into the overall moral calculus.

Despite what we see in the movies, being pregnant isn't like wearing a pink jacket for nine months. It's a transformative, dangerous undertaking like no other. And as such, deserves significant moral weight.

---

33 "The Moral Permissibility of Abortion," page 152.

34 For wisdom on navigating emotionally-charged counterfactuals, see *Midlife: A Philosophical Guide* by Kieran Setiya, Princeton University Press, 2017.

Chapter 7
The UDH's Value

Bioethicist Mary Anne Warren once noted that some seem to view abortion further from unhooking a violinist and "closer to being a morally neutral act, like cutting one's hair."[35] How could anyone equate something as consequential as abortion with a haircut? Because UDHs aren't full persons.

Personhood is a moral designation that applies only to beings possessing special capacities. Lists vary, but typically include the ability to feel pleasure and pain, consciousness, the ability to engage in relationships, and the capacity for rational thought, which makes autonomy, choice and responsibility possible.

The Natural Moral Hierarchy

Notice how the presence or absence of these capacities seems to be connected to how we naturally value things. All else equal, it's more wrong to kill a dog than a butterfly, more wrong to kill a butterfly than a flower. The reason is that dogs are closer to persons than butterflies, and butterflies closer to persons than flowers.

---

35 "On the Moral and Legal Status of Abortion," *The Monist*, Vol 57, No. 1, Women's Liberation: Ethical, Social, and Political Issue (January, 1973), page 52.

Flowers are alive, but they can't feel. Butterflies have a simple neural network that enables a dim awareness, possibly sensations we might recognize as pleasure and pain. But dogs have nervous systems very similar to our own.

We can't get inside Rufus's head and see the world through his eyes. But given our relatively similar anatomy, dogs presumably experience life much as we do. They can think, make basic decisions and as every dog lover knows, form basic relationships. Dogs can experience not only physical pleasure and pain, but emotional joy and anguish which we can infer from their expressions and behavior. A dog's consciousness is more sensitive and sophisticated than a butterfly's, and we rightly rank them higher on the moral scale. Our rankings hold even when the examples are noxious. Killing a mouse seems more wrong than swatting a wasp, and swatting a wasp more wrong than uprooting poison ivy.

Adding a layer of understanding, animal ethicist Tom Regan argued that all normal adult mammals deserve serious moral consideration because they are "subjects-of-a-life."[36] Dogs, cats, deer and monkeys are conscious, feel and are aware that they're a separate entity with unique interests. They know cause and effect ("If I chew through the Christmas lights again, Matt will be disappointed"). They

---

[36] *The Case for Animal Rights,* University of California Press, 2004.

form relationships with family, pack members and even other species. And from their perspective, avoiding pain, pursuing pleasure, acting on their drives and carrying out a good life is of the utmost importance. As Regan puts it:

> [Normal adult mammals] have beliefs and desires; perception, memory, and a sense of the future, including their own future; an emotional life together with feelings of pleasure and pain; preference- and welfare-interests; the ability to initiate action in pursuit of their desires and goals; a psychophysical identity over time; and an individual welfare in the sense that their experiential life fares well or ill for them.[37]

The Importance of Autonomy

We're also subjects-of-a-life. Yet we stand atop the moral kingdom because we're also capable of rational thought and autonomous action. While dogs, cats, deer and monkeys are a result of their environments and experiences, we possess the power of self-change. We can reflect on the sorts of persons we currently are, form and execute plans to become better.[38] Hedonists delay gratification, smokers quit,

---

37 Ibid, page 243.

38 Philosopher Harry Frankfurt explained this in terms of or our ability to have desires about desires ("2nd-order desires") and to take steps to change them. "I want to become the sort of person who *wants* to find solutions rather than problems" can, over time, become a reality.

lazy people get fit. That's autonomy in action.

At one time, I lacked the stamina for prolonged reading. But having realized I needed it to pursue my love of philosophy, I made the decision to develop the habit and did. At one time, I was afraid of physical confrontation, which had caused some cowardly behavior in my youth and lingering shame as an adult. But desiring redemption and with only one life to live, I pushed myself to join a boxing gym and competitively fight.[39]

Monkeys may build banana-peeling skills. Puppies may calm as they mature. But they're driven by genetics, instinct and circumstance. We, on the other hand, can reflect on the sorts of persons we want to be and make our vision a reality. We're no doubt influenced by factors beyond our control. And our transformational power has limits. But our rational capacities facilitate a freedom other creatures lack.

Our autonomy also enables us to be full members of the moral community. Non-human mammals may be subjects-of-a-life. But they can't reflect on the right thing to do and be motivated to do it simply because it's right. Through punishment and reward, I can train a dog to sit, stay, stop eating the Christmas decorations (eventually). But dogs lack a complex sense of morality. They can't weigh the

---

"Desire," Stanford Encyclopedia of Philosophy, revised Apr 9, 2015. https://plato.stanford.edu/entries/desire/

39 Yes, really. See *Year of the Fighter: Lessons from my Midlife Crisis Adventure*, Notaed Press, 2018.

interests at stake if they do X or Y, consider the rational power of arguments for and against X and Y, and choose to do X instead of Y because it's morally best. Only full persons can do that.

Notice that this emphasis on autonomy isn't an irrational privileging of our own kind—it isn't naked speciesism. If it were, we'd prioritize the "human" aspect of UDH rather than the capacities most humans, barring accident, illness or genetic abnormalities, possess. But if the question is which entities are most morally valuable, it makes sense to prioritize those with the power to conduct moral valuations in the first place. In fact, maybe we should grant entities with the mere *potential* to develop this power high moral status.

Potentiality Arguments

John Noonan argued that a UDH's ability to become a full person grants it high moral value from the moment of conception. The genetic code possessed by any normal human blastocyst, zygote or embryo is the primary biological ingredient necessary to develop autonomy, which no other species can boast. As Noonan puts it:

> [A]t conception the new being receives the genetic code. It is this genetic information which determines his characteristics, which is the biological carrier of the possibility of human wisdom, which makes him

a self-evolving being.[40]

Noonan uses the language of "humanization" and "human wisdom." But what he's really saying is that the capacity to develop rationality and autonomy makes UDHs uniquely valuable.

Edward Langerak added that it's not just possession of that genetic code that's key, but the fact that the code is possessed by a being that will, if allowed and nurtured, realize its instruction.

> A potential person is not simply a set of blueprints, it is an organism that itself will become the actual person toward which it is already developing.[41]

Some criticize potentiality arguments on grounds that the potential to become something isn't the same as being that thing. Actual presidents may enjoy the power to pardon crimes. But potential presidents can only commit crimes.[42]

However, the argument isn't that a potential person is *the same* as an actual person. Rather, it's that the potential

---

40 "An Almost Absolute Value in History," from *The Morality of Abortion: Legal and Historical Perspectives*, Harvard University Press, 1970, PDF excerpt page 13.
41 "Abortion: Listening to the Middle," *The Hastings Center Report*, Vol. 9, No. 5 (Oct., 1979), page 25.
42 Credit to Don Marquis, author of the famous "Future Like Ours" argument against abortion, for the presidential example. "An Argument That Abortion is Wrong," *Ethics in Practice: An Anthology* edited by Hugh LaFollette, Wiley & Sons, 2006, page 144.

to become a full person generates some degree of moral value—perhaps a high degree.

Similarly, once the sperm and egg conjoin to create a unique human genetic code, a normal UDH's potential to become a full person justifies granting it heightened moral value, too. However, something interesting happens over the course of pregnancy.

Gradualist Arguments

While potentiality arguments help explain our intuition that UDHs possess some (perhaps high) moral value, gradualist arguments help explain why late-term abortions are more problematic than early term abortions.

While the UDH may be alive from conception, it gradually becomes more person-like and more likely to develop into a full person as it grows. This makes it more morally valuable over the course of development.

Potential presidents are treated similarly. Once a Democrat or Republican primary candidate becomes their party's official nominee, they gain access to deeper campaign funds, are showered (or pelted) with heightened media attention and are eligible to receive classified briefings. Candidates who run a successful campaign have their status elevated yet again between the November election and inauguration in January. The "president-elect" is so close to becoming the Commander in Chief that they get respect from foreign leaders, lobbyists, the press and Secret Service.

Presidential candidates become more likely to become an actual president as they graduate from primary hopeful to party nominee to president-elect. However, they don't fundamentally change. They may soften their message for a general electorate once through the primaries. And most adopt a conciliatory, "We're all Americans—let's come together" tone if they win. But they're still essentially the same creature.

UDHs navigating gestation, on the other hand, not only become more likely to survive into realized persons, but they also develop actual features of personhood. Langerak argued that a UDH's value accordingly increases at four recognizable stages:

> **I - Implantation**: Doctors estimate that more than half of all conceived UDHs never attach to the uterine wall. Without that anchor and nourishment, ceased development and spontaneous miscarriage are the result. Therefore, while alive and human from conception, implantation significantly increases the probability that the UDH will grow into a full person.
>
> **II - Quickening**: "When the [UDH] begins making perceptible spontaneous movements (around the beginning of the second trimester), its shape, its behavior, and even its beginning relationship with

the mother and the rest of society (every father recalls when he first felt the [UDH's] movements) all suggest that abortions after this point will have personal and social consequences specifiably more serious than those of earlier abortions."[43]

III - Viability: Occurs "when a [UDH] is capable of living, with simple medical care, outside the womb (around the end of the second trimester)."[44]

IV - Birth

I'm not convinced Langerak's landmarks are the best. On number four, birth, if we're basing value increases on survival probabilities and burgeoning capacities, it's unclear why a developed, viable UDH nearing delivery would have less value than a birthed baby. We might also replace quickening with the point at which the UDH's nervous system is mature enough for it to feel pleasure and pain. But whatever developmental points we choose, Langerak's approach helps make sense of the way we intuitively judge actual cases, such as:

D: Daniela's pregnancy is the result of rape and she has waited until 23 weeks gestational age to request an abortion.

L: [The UDH has Tay-Sachs disease and] the lab

43 "Abortion: Listening to the Middle," page 27.
44 "Abortion: Listening to the Middle," page 27.

mistakenly delayed release of Latoya's amniocentesis results until 23 weeks gestational age.

Maybe you concluded that since the pregnancy in D is the result of rape, and since the resulting child's life in L would be short and progressively debilitating (due to Tay-Sachs), abortion would be justifiable and/or excusable in both regardless of the UDH's gestational age. But Langerak would argue that we would judge these scenarios more problematic when compared to similar cases where the abortion was sought sooner.

Langerak's primary focus is potentiality and probability. But he does allude to the relevance of actually possessing certain capacities during pregnancy as well.

> If a [UDH] is destroyed, one destroys a being already possessed of the genetic code, organs, and sensitivity to pain, and one which had an 80 percent chance of developing further into a baby outside the womb who, in time, would reason.

Just as we ranked flowers, butterflies and dogs according to which, how many and to what extent they possessed features of personhood, we should do the same for early, middle and late-term UDHs. And a key difference is that barring genetic abnormalities UDHs have the additional ability to become full persons, possessing rationality and an autonomy eventually enabling full membership in the moral community.

Rather than declaring UDHs just as valuable as adults or just as worthless as hair, an informed gradation is more appropriate. Due to their special potential, normal UDHs always have *some* value. And due to the increasing likelihood that they'll realize that potential, and their gradual development of the actual features of personhood, that value increases over the course of gestation. This is consistent with the way we rank non-human entities, as well as with our intuitive judgments on cases earlier or later in pregnancy.

The above are reasons to value UDHs for their own sake, largely as a matter of rational consistency. If we're correct about why mammals are more valuable than insects, insects more valuable than plants and you and I more valuable than all three, then we should use similar logic to appropriately value UDHs. But there's also a case to be made that we should consider what sort of life a UDH is expected to live if it matures into an actual child.

Chapter 8

The Child's Quality of Life

Life can be filled with adventure and love, flourishing and fun. It can also be filled with drudgery and disappointment, misery and pain. While we accept some bad, we expect much good, and usually err on the side of prolonging life whenever possible. However, there are rare occasions when ending a life, especially to avoid or cease great suffering, can be wise and merciful. Consider the fate of the prisoners in the following scenario:

> One by one they were being taken to a nearby steam locomotive, with the firebox roaring, and they were executed by being thrust, headfirst, into the firebox. One of the captives had a few cyanide pills. He gave all but one of these to his friends, who accepted and used them gratefully. He kept one for himself. Then he spied a young boy, also one who was to be killed, shaking in terror. He gave his last pill to the young boy, electing to be killed in the firebox himself.[45]

Bioethicist Richard Brandt uses this story to argue how similar reasoning might apply to babies born with

---

45 "Defective Newborns and the Morality of Termination," from *Infanticide and the Value of Life*, edited by Marvin Kohl, Prometheus Books, 1978, reprinted in *Morality and Moral Controversies, 8th Edition*, edited by Arthur and Scalet, page 266.

painful, hopeless conditions. Allowing a baby to die, or even painlessly hastening its death, is a terrible thing to consider. But just as the man in the story endured the train's firebox for the sake of the boy, choosing to end a doomed baby's life could be similarly heroic, albeit also similarly excruciating.

However, the idea that certain lives may not be worth living seems callous. What appears to be an unacceptable existence to us might be quite acceptable to another. Isn't it arrogant to suggest some would be better off dead? Isn't any life better than *no* life?

Quality of Life Thresholds

Notice how the factors we've considered so far have come in degrees. Conception can be more or less consensual. The mother's interests can be more or less at risk. The value of the UDH can be higher or lower depending on its stage of development. Similarly, prospects for the child's quality of life can be better or worse.

To the extent we expect a child to enjoy a healthy, happy life, it's more difficult to justify aborting. But to the extent we expect a child to suffer a stunted, painful life, the case for a mercy abortion strengthens.

Imagine if we could predict left-handedness. Lefties have a tougher time buying scissors, baseball gloves and guitars. As my left-handed wife and youngest son can attest, this can be an annoying inconvenience. But it isn't annoying enough to make lefty lives not worth living.

However, consider Cases K and L, where amniocentesis reveals the UDH has Tay-Sachs Disease, "a fatal genetic condition which causes the progressive loss of senses and mobility, eventually leading to paralysis and death in early childhood." If that's not enough, add a diagnosis of spina bifida myelomeningocele, a condition where the spinal cord protrudes between separated vertebrae, causing pain and in some cases paralysis of the legs.[46] Or combine these conditions with severe mental and other physical handicaps.

If we compound enough congenital issues, at some point, life stops being worth living. Whatever that threshold is, when it's crossed, the compassionate thing to do is to spare a UDH from suffering such an awful existence. This isn't a fun prospect to consider, especially for a parent. And I can't imagine having to make such a tragic decision. But it seems the honest, mature decision nonetheless.

An Unstable Home?

Recall that Case B stipulated that Bianca was a known prostitute. Why did the original Rate That Abortion authors include that detail? Perhaps to invite reflection on the child's

---

[46] https://www.cdc.gov/ncbddd/spinabifida/facts.html and https://www.mayoclinic.org/diseases-conditions/spina-bifida/symptoms-causes/syc-20377860 Note that in-utero surgical treatments of spina bifida are advancing.

life prospects.

Given the sometimes violent and dangerous nature of sex work, it seems fair to assume a prostitute would have a diminished ability to maintain a healthy pregnancy. And given the unfortunate circumstances that drive many people to become sex workers, including addiction, poverty, desperation and abuse, it's less likely a sex worker would be able to provide a quality homelife, at least compared to a factory worker, accountant or surgeon.[47]

Could a sex worker's UDH's future be *so* dim to warrant a mercy abortion automatically? I wouldn't think so. However, if we add that the woman is trapped in a war-torn country, has AIDS, lacks access to prenatal care, is homeless, can barely feed herself, etc., we might conclude exactly that.

Could circumstances be so dire that they decrease the UDH's chances of becoming a full person at all? Yes. Imagine a famine-stricken area with a 90% infant mortality rate—maybe Ethiopia in the mid-80s or regions of Syria during their civil war. Reasons in favor of bringing a UDH to term might still prevail. And it might retain some innate, genetic-based potential to become a full person. But its real-world prospects could make that symbolic possibility moot.

---

47 There are, of course, exceptions. But it seems fair to assume most prostitutes didn't rationally choose their occupation from a long list of attractive options.

With the UDH's health and the resulting child's quality of life in mind, revisit Case GG where mother Gabby is a heroin addict, as well as Case C where Celeste is thirteen. You might conclude that any life is better than no life, and that we shouldn't pretend to own a crystal ball. All I'm arguing is that reasonable and informed expectations about the child's quality of life are relevant. How much weight to assign that factor remains an open question.

Responsible Decision-Making

When Pam received harsh medications to treat dysentery, doctors predicted her son would be born with birth defects so severe his life wouldn't be worth living. They advised her to abort to save him that fate.

But not only was Pam Tebow's son, Tim, a healthy child, he became a healthy enough adult to lead the University of Florida Gators to two national championships and the Denver Broncos to the NFL playoffs.[48]

These sorts of mistakes, no matter how rare, shake the public's faith in physicians' predictions. Hear of enough of them, and you may be tempted to replace sober analysis with wishful thinking.

There's nothing wrong with hoping for a miracle and even allowing some time for one to occur. But when you've

---

48 "Fact Check: Tim Tebow's Birth Story" by Carole Fader, January, 2012, The Florida Times-Union, https://www.jacksonville.com/article/20120107/NEWS/801259737.

received second and third opinions, and after careful reflection, parents must make the best decisions they can with the best information available.

This is gut-wrenchingly tragic. But holding out in the face of overwhelming evidence is irresponsible. We can empathize with parents placed in such a terrible situation. We can understand and forgive decision delays. But we still know that when continuing a pregnancy will facilitate immeasurable suffering, the mature choice can be a mercy termination.

Left-handedness wouldn't be reason enough. What about Down Syndrome, which causes developmental delays and heart issues, but doesn't preclude an overall happy life? How terrible a UDH's life prospects would need to be to justify a mercy abortion, I'll leave for you to ponder. But the point here is that such a threshold does exist, and is yet another consideration to factor into the overall moral calculus.

Chapter 9
The Father's Autonomy

Sometimes fathers express firm and strong abortion preferences. Some insist an abortion should happen. Some insist an abortion should *not* happen.

But even if we allow men to join the abortion discussion, shouldn't we exclude their interests from actual abortion decisions? After all, the father's contribution is hardly burdensome. Why should his wishes matter?

What weight should we grant a father's input? And on what grounds might we acknowledge or dismiss it? One approach is to consider procreation an exercise of autonomy.

Honoring Reasonable Expectations

College degrees don't fall out of the sky. To earn one, students must maintain a quality high school GPA, study for and do well enough on entrance exams, arrange for financing and complete an array of paperwork simply to begin. Then they have to endure Freshman English and possibly Stats, declare a major, satisfy distribution requirements, fill out graduation forms and pay various fees, all according to inflexible deadlines. Yet, determined people find a way.

However, no one earns a college degree alone. Even

the most self-reliant students need professors to assess them fairly, administrators to track their progress, tech professionals to sustain course websites and keep grade databases from crashing. They also need the school to honor reasonable and steady terms.

If a college changed its requirements days before graduation, students would rightly protest. After investing so much time, effort and money, they would expect the original agreement to be honored. Lawyers might help the school get away with it. But if a student had been led to believe that passing certain courses within a certain time would entitle them to a certain degree, they could rightly complain that the school's bait-and-switch undermined their autonomy.

George Harris makes a structurally similar fatherhood argument.[49] Just as students deserve to have their reasonable expectations concerning college honored, men deserve to have their reasonable expectations concerning procreation honored. Harris insists men who invest their time, emotions, and finances in a relationship under the reasonable impression their partner will bear their child deserve to have that expectation upheld.

Harris illustrates his argument through five fictitious cases. In the first (which I call Recovered Rapist), a temporarily insane man rapes a woman, is cured and begs

---

49 "Fathers and Fetuses," *Ethics 96* (1986), University of Chicago Press.

her to maintain the pregnancy. Harris argues that the woman has no responsibility to do so, since the rapist overrode and disrespected *her* autonomy.

In the second (which I call Closet Catholic—these are all my labels, not Harris's), a couple has casual sex, and when the woman becomes pregnant, the man suddenly reveals his devout Catholicism. He pleads with her to maintain the pregnancy, even offering to cover all medical expenses and raise the child himself. She refuses, aborts, and Harris says this is OK because the man could not have reasonably assumed the woman would be willing to bear his child if accidentally impregnated. Since the man never shared his reservations against abortion (Catholics are generally anti-abortion), there's no way the woman could have known, and she, therefore, made no implied agreement to bear his children.

The third case (Secret Confusion), involves a married couple who agree to have kids together someday. While the man makes it clear that having children is *the* most important thing to him, the woman is secretly unsure whether she wants kids at all. She gets pregnant at a time when carrying could cost her a promotion at work and decides to abort. Harris argues this is unfortunate but permissible because it's understandable that a wife might be afraid to share her doubts about raising a family. Plus, pursuing her career is essential to her autonomy, and Harris is ambivalent on whether the man's or woman's autonomy is more important in this case.

The fourth case (Secret Aversion) is similar to the third, except the wife secretly *knows* she doesn't want children. Harris argues that in this case the woman has a moral obligation to maintain the pregnancy since aborting would severely and knowingly infringe on the man's autonomy—would damage, disrupt and undermine his life plans, which he explicitly communicated and she agreed to support. I'm not so sure about Harris's analysis on this one, which we'll explore further in a moment.

Finally, the fifth case (Gender Avenger) involves a woman who intentionally seduces and marries a man desperate to start a family in order to exact revenge on all men for their historical oppression of women. She pretends to love him and share his deep desire to start a family. But then relishes his horror when she reveals her plot. She gleefully aborts, breaking his heart in the process, without the slightest remorse.

Is Harris Correct?

Harris argues, and I agree, that the last case, Gender Avenger, is the most blatantly unethical. But one thing to consider with the second case, Closet Catholic, is whether it was unreasonable for the man to believe that his casual sex partner would carry if accidentally impregnated.

Harris implies that the man's devout Catholicism is an oddity in need of disclosure, and the woman's comparative comfort aborting the default expectation. However, the couple could have been classmates at a Catholic university, met at church, or simply lived in a culture where abortion is frowned upon. The casual nature of their relationship suggests neither party should assume the other is seriously committed *to them.* But their lack of commitment to one another seems independent of what we might fairly assume about their views on abortion.

With Secret Confusion and Secret Aversion, the wives deceive their husbands, or at least allow them to continue to believe an important untruth. In both cases, the men believe the women intend to bear and help raise their children. Harris argues that since the woman was only unsure about having her husband's children in Secret Confusion, her failure to disclose that uncertainty largely absolves her from blame and renders aborting permissible. But with Secret Aversion, since the woman knew she was prolonging a dead-end relationship and faking support for the man's central life goal, her harm to his autonomy is more egregious, rendering that abortion impermissible.

Harris thinks whether the woman was secretly unsure or secretly unsupportive determines whether aborting would be permissible. However, note how the husband's autonomy is equally harmed independent of the wife's internal mind states. In both cases, Harris stipulates that starting a family is *the* most important thing to the husband. In both cases, the man will have to start over with another relationship, the time wasted with the first woman deducted from the time left for living his dream of being a family man. In both cases, the men's plans have been equally derailed, their autonomy equally undermined.

To see this, consider a professor unsure of whether she'll implement a new grading scale that will flunk fifteen students who would have otherwise passed. She believes the new scale would combat grade inflation, but is conflicted on whether and when to adopt it. In the second case, the professor *knows* she's going to implement the new grading scale, and knows it will cause fifteen students to fail, but keeps her plan secret.

In the final week of the semester, both professors carry out the grading change, and as a result, thirty additional students fail (fifteen in each class). It seems the students who would have otherwise passed have had their autonomy equally disrespected, independent of whether their professor was secretly undecided or simply secretive.

Maybe the confusion of the professor in the first case makes her less blameworthy—maybe it's understandable that she wouldn't want to reveal her grade inflation worries, which might distract or anger her students. But from the perspective of the students, their GPAs are equally impacted, their autonomy equally undermined, regardless of whether they had had the misfortune of studying under the first or second professor.

It seems the husbands in Secret Confusion and Secret Aversion have their autonomy equally infringed in a similar way, which would seem to make both abortions equally problematic. As we know, one factor alone doesn't settle the morality of an abortion. But the point here is that the biological father's interests are relevant, especially insofar as it's reasonable for him to believe that, should his partner become pregnant, she will gestate the resulting UDH.

Hardwig's Counter

Harris helps us appreciate a father's legitimate interest in a UDH's survival. However, bioethicist John Hardwig offers an argument in the other direction, inviting us to consider a father's interest in a UDH's termination.

At the heart of it are what others have dubbed the "burdens of biological parenthood." Even though fathers don't suffer the difficulties of pregnancy, when a man procreates, he implicitly accepts some responsibility for his offspring's care. This is the partial basis for laws that saddle fathers with financial obligations. Even if otherwise out of the picture, they're still expected to support their children's material wellbeing. But when an unwanted UDH gestates without the father's approval, this not only puts him at risk for child support debt, but can generate future guilt over unfulfilled duties.

Hardwig argues that since it would be unsettling to know that an unwanted child is wandering the earth without your mentoring, protection and love, fathers should be allowed to insist that a UDH be aborted to avoid this mental strain. A woman should never be *forced* to abort. As Hardwig puts it, "How would that even work? The mind balks and the stomach turns."[50] But mothers should voluntarily honor an unwanting father's wishes—he should be granted veto power over whether a UDH lives, in the name of allowing him to avoid the dread of knowing a person he created is facing life without him.

> A pregnant woman who is planning to have a child over the objections of the biological father or without his knowledge is wronging him... By making him a father against his wishes, she is altering his life and inflicting a serious harm to perfectly legitimate interests of his.[51]

Is Hardwig Correct?

Hardwig is right to highlight how an abandoned UDH can haunt a father. But notice that the same reasons he

---

50 "Men & Abortion Decisions," page 44.
51 "Men & Abortion Decisions," *Hasting Center Report* 45, no. 2 (2015), page 42.

offers for aborting a UDH could be offered to justify killing a child. If the father of a ten-year-old were to say, "I'm feeling especially guilty for not caring for my son, so I think he should be killed," we'd of course object. Hardwig's argument is therefore only plausible if we assume a low valuation of the UDH—low enough to be overridden by an unwanting father's mental anguish.

However, there's a tension in this reasoning. To the extent a biological father would be haunted by unfulfilled paternal obligations, this suggests a high moral valuation of their offspring. After all, if fathers don't owe their children love and care, abandoning them wouldn't produce guilt-like anguish. But to the extent a father acknowledges parental obligations and expects their future unfulfillment to be burdensome, this suggests the UDH is actually very valuable, and that the father should advocate that it be brought to term rather than aborted.

Hardwig could reply that we're guilty of equivocating here. Perhaps parental obligations don't trigger until after a UDH becomes a birthed baby, such that an abortion can be a way to nip them in the bud. Maybe fathers can owe their birthed babies a great deal, but their UDHs very little.

Noonan and Langerak would respond that since a UDH already possesses the genetic code to become the father's birthed child, and since it's already on the trajectory toward becoming that child, some parental obligations kick in long before birth. However, consistent with the gradualist view, perhaps those obligations would be lower earlier in pregnancy, since an early-term UDH wouldn't yet be conscious or able to feel.

A key question would become, which is weightier: the objective value of a UDH plus the strength of parental obligations to them? Or the anguish an unwanting father anticipates suffering if his UDH is brought to term? If the father's concern about future mental anguish were the only or primary reason in favor of aborting, it wouldn't seem powerful enough.

Hardwig's argument also seems to inflate the importance of being raised by your genetic parents. While life without your biological father might be less enjoyable than one with him, surely life can be good enough, as millions of sons and daughters of single mothers, stepfathers and adoptive dads can attest.

The bottom line is that while some guilt over unfulfilled parental responsibilities would seem appropriate, it wouldn't seem severe enough to warrant terminating. And in any case, a father concerned with his future child's wellbeing would seem to have more reason to oppose an abortion than insist on one.

We've actually discussed this, and Hardwig isn't convinced the burdens on the father can be reduced to mental anguish. To some extent, the career and life prospect risks inflicted on mothers also apply to fathers. Even the health risks apply if the father has a dangerous job—mining coal or deploying to Afghanistan to support his newly birthed child.[52]

On the career and finance front, Hardwig is correct. Child support payments would impact him materially, not simply mentally, constraining his employment options and income. However, on the emotional front, fathers can always choose guilt over involvement. But this is exactly the situation Hardwig wants to avoid—children lacking loving dads and men regretting the encounter that made them a father.

My point is simply that a life without your genetic dad is better than no life at all, and that a father's anticipated shame and wage garnishments aren't enough to override the value of a potential person. Especially if we think there's a link between choices and responsibility, fathers shouldn't be able to insist that a UDH conceived via voluntary sex be aborted.

---

[52] Correspondence October, 2020, cleared with John for publication.

Chapter 10
Third Parties

Whether wealthy or broke, healthy or sick, gay or straight, people tend to prefer policies that benefit them personally. Even when we *try* to be objective, rich black men wind up preferring policies that advantage rich black men. Working-class whites wind up preferring policies that benefit working-class whites.

This presents a problem. Our conclusions are supposed to be the product of logic, not power. However, what if there were a way to transcend our clouding biases?

The Golden Veil

Out of the corner of your eye you spot a luxurious gold curtain floating in mid-air. Across the top reads a mysterious Lord of the Rings-style inscription. It's not written in a recognizable language. But somehow you know it says, "Veil of Ignorance."

Curious, you pull it aside and step past. A flash of light dims to a soft glow. You know you were just reading about abortion ethics. But you can't remember where you were. In fact, you can't remember much of anything about yourself—your name, race, gender, income, occupation, education, religious commitments, political allegiances, handicaps, talents, hobbies, passions, phobias. Not even your favorite flavor of ice cream.

Holding up a hand to inspect your skin color, you can only see a shade of gray. Feeling your body to determine your sex, your brain won't say.

Dumbfounded, yet oddly at peace, you see that I've followed you. We both admit an overwhelming desire to discuss abortion. But we can't remember if we're generally for or against it, what our family and colleagues expect us to think about it or how we ourselves might be impacted by it.

You suggest that we revisit the Rate That Abortion exercise. We do, and while we're happy with our scores, they're definitely different than before.

We discuss the nature of the conception, the mother's interests, the UDH's value, the child's quality of life and the father's autonomy. On some level, we want our conclusions to benefit us personally. But blocked from knowing who we are, we're prevented from gaming the analysis in our favor.

Recognizing that personal preferences should have no bearing on morality, we agree that whatever we decide behind this magic golden veil should govern our views when we return to the real world. We know that we may not *like* what we've decided here. But we shake hands nonetheless, promising to promote whatever conclusions we've drawn from this enlightened perspective.

20th century American political philosopher John

Rawls designed this "Original Position" thought experiment as a sort of reasoning machine.[53] Issues go in, more objective than usual answers come out. His primary focus was the basic structure of society, or what a nation's constitution would ideally guarantee. But the method can be applied to any issue, including abortion.

I'll save the full exposition of Rawls for *Political Philosophy in a Nutshell* (forthcoming 2025, maybe?). The idea here is to offer his approach as a supplement. If you didn't know if you were male or female, Republican or Democrat, Baptist or Agnostic, rape victim or expecting father, how might your analyses change?

In fact, how might your analyses change if you didn't know if you were an impacted third party? Everyone's interests should matter *some.* The question is, how much?

Family

Consider Case M, where another child would put Michaela and Michael's struggling family at risk of homelessness. Should the potential consequences for children Miranda, Melanie, Matthew and Martin matter?

In H, Hannah has invasive cervical cancer. A prompt

---

53 Rawls wrote several books, but for a thirty-page synopsis see his "Justice as Fairness: Political not Metaphysical," *Philosophy and Public Affairs*, Vol. 14, No. 3. (Summer, 1985) pages 223-251. Or find my twenty-minute lecture vid on Sandel's *Justice:* Chapter 6 at youtube.com/MattDeatonPhD

hysterectomy would give her a good chance of surviving. But while she wants to forego the procedure to save the UDH, husband Henry is encouraging her to abort and begin chemo, insisting that he and their three existing children, Holly, Harry and Helio, need her to live.

In DD, Dacia considers aborting to take a long-planned trip around the world, which wouldn't be as safe or enjoyable if pregnant. Of course, she could delay it. But as the case specifies, this would cause her to lose a significant deposit, and it's understood that circumnavigating the globe is harder and more expensive with a child, though also possibly more fun and fulfilling.

How we decide DD depends largely on the value of the UDH vs. the deposit plus assumptions on how having a child (or another child) would impact the trip. However, EE adds an interesting twist.

> Same as (DD), except Eva will be accompanied by her mother Esther who is dying of cancer and whose last wish is to take this trip with Eva.

We might suggest Eva hire a traveling midwife to oversee delivery and care for the baby. Or if it's early enough, remove and cryogenically freeze the UDH, re-implanting and bringing it to term after the trip. However, even if Eva could afford it, this probably isn't medically possible today. So if we're stuck with these depressing details—and for the purposes of philosophical thought experiments, we're stuck with the depressing details—we must choose between the value of the UDH and honoring her mother Esther's dying wish.

This gives us pause—more pause than Dacia's substantial deposit in DD—for a once-in-a-lifetime experience with a cherished loved one is indeed weightier than a sum of cash.

However, that's assuming Eva and mother Esther have a good relationship. Just because we share a biological connection with someone doesn't mean we must honor their desires. Toxic family members sometimes deserve to be ostracized, their wishes ignored. And as every child of a loving stepparent knows, sometimes the strongest family ties involve no blood relation at all.

The point: family members—good and involved family members, at least—deserve to have their interests weighted. As much as the mother's? Of course not. As much as the father's? Probably not, though if the father has proven uninterested, a supportive grandparent, aunt or cousin might deserve a weightier say. But what about complete strangers? Do we have reason to factor in the interests of people we don't know at all?

Public Safety

Every UDH is a potential president, philanthropist or astronaut. Maybe they'll cure cancer or do something truly impressive, like becoming a world-class violinist.

However, as Stephen J. Dubner and Steven Levitt argue in *Freakenomics: A Rogue Economist Explores the Hidden Side of Everything,*[54] every UDH is also a potential villain. Rather than contributing great good, they may cause great harm. And after some statistical analysis, Dubner and Levitt conclude that abortions are apparently more likely to screen out future law-breakers than future do-gooders.

A key finding was that per capita crime in the US went down after Roe v. Wade, suggesting that wider availability to abortion prevented the birth of many would-be criminals. Why? One explanation is that parents who seek abortions often do so because they believe they're ill-prepared to nurture a child. Since a rocky childhood can lead to a rocky adulthood, allowing parents to abort prevents that rocky life altogether. But when abortion isn't an option, many parents wind up raising children they don't want and can't properly support.

Some rise to the challenge. Parenting can make a person more patient, compassionate and empathetic. This has been my experience, though I also still say and do things I regret and make my share of mistakes. But some parents

---

54 Published by William Morrow, 2005.

don't rise to the challenge, and while kids from supportive families (like mine) still sometimes get into trouble with the law (like I did), and neglected, abused children certainly aren't destined for a life of crime, it's reasonable to think a less stable and supportive homelife would make a child more prone to break the law as an adult.[55]

Does *Freakenomics* Work?

Around the same time Roe went into effect, so did the un-leading of gasoline. As Dubner and Levitt concede, elevated lead levels have been associated with learning difficulties and criminal behavior. And so maybe crime dropped after widespread abortion was legalized not because many would-be law-breakers were aborted, but because many would-be law-breakers' nervous systems weren't poisoned by dirty gas.

However, in an attempt to isolate the impact of Roe and the de-leading of gasoline, the authors also compared crime rates among states based on how difficult abortions had been to obtain.[56] Their conclusion: the easier it was to get

---

55 See the "Delinquency and Crime" section of *New Directions in Child Abuse and Neglect,* Committee on Child Maltreatment Research, Policy, and Practice for the Next Decade: Phase II; Board on Children, Youth, and Families; Committee on Law and Justice; Institute of Medicine; National Research Council; Petersen AC, Joseph J, Feit M, editors. Washington (DC): National Academies Press (US); 2014 Mar 25. https://www.ncbi.nlm.nih.gov/books/NBK195987/

56 Even after the Roe decision, pro-life advocates continued to lobby legislatures to curtail abortion access, and have been more or less successful in different states.

an abortion in a given state, the less crime that state was likely to suffer per capita.

> For the period from 1973-1988, the two sets of states (high abortion states and low abortion states) have nearly identical crime patterns. Note, that this is a period *before* the generations exposed to legalized abortion are old enough to do much crime… But from the period 1985-1997, when the post Roe cohort is reaching peak crime ages, the high abortion states see a decline in crime of 30% relative to the low abortion states.[57]

Their reasonable conclusion: while un-leading gasoline may have helped decrease crime, there's reason to believe wider access to abortion did as well.

As you might expect, *Freakenomics* drew widespread criticism.[58] However, even if abortion were shown to decrease crime, would that alone be good reason to support it?

Probably not. Just because something might boost the economy, improve test scores, decrease crime, etc. doesn't mean it's morally best, or even morally permissible. Reinstituting slavery might do wonders for the economy.

---

57 "Abortion and Crime: Who Should You Believe?" by Steven D. Levitt, May 15, 2005, *Freakenomics Blog*. https://freakonomics.com/2005/05/15/abortion-and-crime-who-should-you-believe/

58 See challenges from Steve Sailer and John Lott at the link above.

Flogging bad students might boost test scores. Cutting off thieves' hands might decrease theft. You get the idea.

Further, the authors of *Freakenomics* conceded that to the extent a person believes abortion itself should be criminalized, they're less likely to be impressed that more abortions might decrease other forms of crime. Even if the trade-off worked, only people who didn't consider abortion a big deal would care.

The book presents an interesting empirical argument, the plausibility of which I'll leave to the statisticians to judge. But I can comfortably say that it doesn't present a conclusive moral argument that abortion is a just form of crime control. In fact, there's a competing argument that abortion is actually bad for society on whole, and particularly bad for women.

Attitudes Toward Women

While some defend the death penalty as an effective crime deterrent, Jeffrey Reiman argues that executing violent criminals does the opposite.[59] Even when carried out in the name of justice, even when the penalty matches the crime, even when dispassionate and sanitized, executions send the message that killing persons is sometimes OK. And

---

59 "Against the Death Penalty," *Ethics in Practice, 3rd Edition,* edited by Hugh LaFollette, Blackwell, 2007, pages 554-561, based on Pojman and Reiman's *The Death Penalty: For and Against,* Rowman and Littlefield, 1998.

over time, this has a cumulative hardening effect on social attitudes.

Nobody hears about an execution and becomes instantly compelled to shoot their neighbor. But state executions move the culture in a more callous, violent direction, which eventually leads to more murder than were human life treated more sacredly. The threat of execution may very well deter some would-be killers. But ultimately the practice causes more murders than it prevents. Or so Reiman argues.

Feminist Sidney Callahan, whom we first met in The Nature of the Conception chapter, makes a similar argument concerning abortion. She argues that on-demand abortion "masculinizes" sex, an approach that has brought "epidemics of venereal disease, infertility, pornography, sexual abuse, adolescent pregnancy, divorce, displaced older women" and reinforces the view that rather than indispensable givers of human life, women are primarily objects of pleasure.[60] Rather than empowering women, abortion erodes their perceived value.

Callahan argues that abortion also suggests sexual irresponsibility is acceptable and that care for pregnant women and mothers isn't necessary. If parenting proves difficult, why should society care? Struggling single moms have only themselves to blame—they should have planned

---

60 "A Case for Pro-Life Feminism," page 122.

ahead and prevented their child's birth. Or so people might conclude in a world in which abortion as birth control is commonplace. As Callahan puts it:

> More and more frequently, we hear some version of this old rationalization: if she refuses to get rid of it, it's her problem. A child becomes a product of the individual woman's freely chosen investment, a form of private property resulting from her own cost-benefit calculation. The larger community is relieved of moral responsibility.[61]

John Hardwig makes a related point concerning men's reaction to women's ability to unilaterally abort.

> [B]y viewing decisions about unwanted pregnancies as exclusively the woman's decision, we teach men that being a father is much less demanding or consuming than being a mother.... [signaling to men that it's OK to] abandon their biological children in a variety of ways, ranging from trying to avoid child-support payments, through emotional unavailability and refusal to exercise visitation rights, down to a complete lack of interest.[62]

That's one paradigm. The other is a world in which romantic love is the norm, where couples treat sex with

---

61 "A Case for Pro-Life Feminism," page 121.
62 "Men & Abortion Decisions," page 44.

seriousness and where pregnant women and mothers are valorized. Callahan argues that UDHs shouldn't be treated as discardable artifacts of oppression or pregnancy a curse. If women instead embraced and celebrated their unique life-giving power, this would actually better promote their collective long-term happiness.

Pro-choice feminists of course reply that access to abortion is essential to gender equality. A sexually active man risks STDs and child support debt. But a sexually active woman risks all of that plus her career, life plans, her identity and health. Access to abortion can partially mitigate this unfairness, allowing women to end unwanted pregnancies similar to how men can walk away from them. Abortion serves as the great gender equalizer, freeing women from the undeserved tyranny of their wombs. Without it, there's no hope for substantive and lasting equality.

Common ground between pro-choice and pro-life feminists would include the desire for more robust support before, during and after pregnancy. But pro-life feminists insist that the benefits of abortion are superficial, far outweighed by the drawbacks.

Like all great debates, there's truth in both views. A person could rationalize that struggling mothers who could have avoided the situation by aborting have less claim to public support. A father who had no say in whether a UDH was brought to term could claim that the child should be hers to care for and hers alone.

At the same time, women do indeed suffer a reproductive unfairness that allows men to enjoy sex with less risk. Parental responsibility laws that empower courts to garnish fathers' wages help. But the impact on her is still disproportionate.

Interestingly, some American states known for most tightly restricting abortion are the same states known for providing the least support to women and children.[63] However, reputation isn't always reality,[64] and the political motives driving policy are mysterious and ad hoc. States stingy toward women and children may simply be stingy in general, and so this doesn't necessarily disprove Callahan's thesis.

Callahan might also respond that simply constraining abortion access shouldn't be expected to make society more caring toward women instantly, any more than banning the death penalty would cut the murder rate instantly. But that rejecting abortion is a necessary ingredient in an enlightened approach promoting the interests of women, just as a moratorium on executions

---

63 "Abortion Policy and Child Well-Being in the United States" by Marshall Medoff, *Health Care for Women International*, Volume 37, 2016, Issue 2, pages 158-169.
64 "Best & Worst States for Working Moms" by John S. Kiernan, *WalletHub*, May 6, 2020. https://wallethub.com/edu/best-states-for-working-moms/3565

could be a necessary ingredient in an enlightened approach promoting public safety.

The Environment?

Sometimes people argue that abortion is good for society because it's good for the environment. How? When we count up each new baby's lifetime contribution to climate change, then add their descendants' carbon footprint as well, not only does abortion decrease pollution, having kids at all is morally problematic.[65] As The Washington Post's Tamar Haspel puts it, "No amount of bean eating or Prius-driving will compensate for reproducing, and it's the childless, not the vegetarians, who are more likely to save the planet."[66]

However, former Atlantic editor Sigal Samuel makes a decent argument that with various countries and states committed to progressively restricting emissions, people born today won't contribute as much harm to the environment as recent generations.[67] Further, any harm an

---

65 "Want to Fight Climate Change? Have Fewer Children," by Damian Carrington for *The Guardian*, July 12, 2017. https://www.theguardian.com/environment/2017/jul/12/want-to-fight-climate-change-have-fewer-children

66 Quoted by Craig Chandler in "How Family Size Shapes Your Carbon Footprint" for Yale Climate Connections, March 29, 2019. https://yaleclimateconnections.org/2019/03/how-family-size-shapes-your-carbon-footprint/

67 "Having Fewer Kids Will Not Save the Environment," VOX, Feb 13, 2020. https://www.vox.com/future-

additional baby might cause can be offset by donating a modest amount to an effective environmental protection advocacy group. She cites a Founders Pledge study that recommends the intergovernmental Coalition for Rainforest Nations and the US-based Clean Air Task Force as two groups especially efficient at reducing CO2, so much so that donating even $100 would do more to decrease emissions than giving up your car and having one fewer child *combined.* The real enemy isn't too many humans. It's humans' reliance on fossil fuels.

Samuel notes how the study authors concede that their calculations assume governments will follow through on promises to reduce emissions, which might not come to fruition. However, even if abortion were shown to help the environment, this alone wouldn't be reason to embrace it.

We could give terrorists a bioweapon and suggest they release it in Paris. If they did, many people would die, and we'd be saved the victims' pollution. We could put the most conspicuous polluters on house arrest, revoke their Amazon privileges and censor their Instagram accounts. Or we could sterilize people whose last name begins with the letter B, capping emissions from new Bocks, Bracketts and Burnetts.

But similar to how crime reduction alone isn't reason

perfect/2020/2/13/21132013/climate-change-children-kids-anti-natalism enough to promote abortion, potentially helping the environment doesn't seem to be, either.

In fact, since the harm abortion causes future generations is more direct, immediate and certain, maybe it's more wrong to abort than to pollute. If we should protect the environment for the sake of humans who won't be born for 100 years, maybe we should be more concerned with the welfare of humans who will be born within the next nine months.

I'll leave for you to decide whether concern for future generations should translate into concern for UDHs, as well as how to weight the potential environmental benefits of more widespread abortions. Reflect on your valuation of UDHs, the seriousness of the climate change problem, whether alternative solutions might address it adequately well and to what extent abortion as an environmental protection might be analogous to other strategies you might or might not endorse.

One difference is that UDHs facing abortion today presumably aren't wanted by their parents, whereas future people, whom we imagine having been born (and driving flying cars), presumably will be wanted by their parents. But another difference is that the UDHs of today have already been conceived.

How ever you decide any of these questions, hopefully you now better appreciate how the interests of third parties can matter, and how "pro-this vs. pro-that" just doesn't cut it. Rather than a straightforward, single-factor issue, abortion is far more complicated than our culture pretends.

For those of us who know the truth, it's natural to wish the equation wasn't so tough. What if it didn't have to be? What if there were a way to reconcile the central tension? What if there were a way to *solve* abortion?

Chapter 11

Abortion Solved?

Blue light bulbs cast an eerie glow around a table in the middle of the room. A velvet drape covered a large object in the center of the table…

Carole smiled. "Would you like to meet one of the next citizens of Klaipeda?" she asked.

Without waiting for his answer, she slowly pulled the drape back. Beneath it sat a glass orb filled with some sort of liquid. In the dim light he could see an object in the liquid.

"We try to simulate the environment in the womb as closely as we can," Carole said. "So the lights in here are always down low." She tapped a key on one of the laptop computers, and soft light from the base of the orb became a little brighter. The light illuminated a mass of skin and veins and tendrils at the bottom of the sphere. A long, vein-covered tube snaked from the bottom of the orb to a tiny [UDH] floating in the center of the sphere.

"Oh, my… Is he alive?"

"Very much so. And he's a she."

- *The 3rd Option* by Ben Sharpton

Ectogenesis, the technology central to Ben Sharpton's novel *The 3rd Option* will someday enable gestation of UDHs outside a mother's womb. Whether the devices look more like glowing orbs or Ziploc bags, as with recent experiments with Unborn Developing Lambs,[68] science fiction will become medical reality—possibly within our lifetimes—and probably by the end of the century. The implications for abortion ethics are tremendous.

Given artificial wombs' potential to honor the interests and values central to both sides of the traditional debate—facilitating choice *and* life—we might expect widespread enthusiasm. Ethicists Peter Singer and Deanne Wells predict that the ability to end pregnancy without terminating the UDH should enable pro-choice and pro-life adversaries to "embrace in happy harmony."[69] However, I've been broaching the idea with colleagues, students, family and friends for more than a decade, and most are skeptical, some downright hostile.

Many people who lean pro-life respond that women should maintain their pregnancies as nature (or God) intended. UDHs are too valuable to trust to a machine,

---

68 "Artificial Womb Keeps Premature Lambs Alive for Weeks. Are Humans Next?" by Ike Swetlitz for PBS, Apr 26, 2017. https://www.pbs.org/newshour/health/artificial-womb-keeps-premature-lambs-alive-weeks-humans-next

69 "Ectogenesis," chapter two of the anthology *Ectogenesis: Artificial Womb Technology and the Future of Human Reproduction* edited by Robert Ginsberg and Peter Redpath, Rodopi, 2006, page 12.

gestation too important to botch. Women should consider the burdens of pregnancy before having sex, and those who become pregnant should accept responsibility for nurturing the vulnerable life within them.

Many people who lean pro-choice respond that UDHs aren't worth the trouble. If a woman wants an abortion for any reason, we should respect her choice and carry it out in full—the UDH not only removed, but terminated. After all, it's only a UDH, it's *her* UDH, and if she wants its development to cease, she should be able to insist as much.[70] Besides, this sounds like another ploy by men to control women. No thank you.

So despite my enthusiasm, if the idea isn't instantly resonating, you're not alone. But for a solution-oriented, peacemaking philosopher tired of the protracted and worsening division—which thanks to our two-party system also impacts environmental policy, national defense, firearms regulations, healthcare and everything else—artificial wombs seem extraordinarily promising.

No one gets what they *thought* they wanted—to force women to remain pregnant or to ensure UDHs are terminated. But everyone gets what they *really* wanted—freedom to end an unwanted pregnancy and the ability to see every healthy UDH grow into a happy child.

---

[70] Next chapter is devoted to analyzing this proposed "right to the UDH's death."

Feminist Disagreement

One way to decide whether artificial wombs would ameliorate or exacerbate the abortion issue is by considering it through various feminist lenses. We already know that while some feminists generally support abortion, some generally oppose it. When it comes to artificial wombs, they're similarly divided. Maureen Sander-Staudt explains why by bucketing feminists into three ideological camps.[71]

Liberal Feminists argue that gender disparities in pay and power are the result of tradition and law, and promote equality through public policy, pushing for nondiscrimination in the workplace, equal pay and wide availability to abortion. If freed from natural gestation, Liberal Feminists argue that artificial wombs could help women pursue educational and career goals, and might encourage society to stop thinking of women as caregivers. This could make women more successful employees and leaders, enabling a life more on par with men. It could also give some infertile women the freedom to have kids and allow women to begin a family after menopause.

Radical Feminists (these are Sander-Staudt's labels, not mine) share Liberal Feminists' goal of gender equality,

[71] "Of Machine Born? A Feminist Assessment of Ectogenesis and Artificial Wombs," chapter eight of the anthology *Ectogenesis: Artificial Womb Technology and the Future of Human Reproduction* edited by Robert Ginsberg and Peter Redpath, Rodopi, 2006, pages 109-127.

but argue that political solutions aren't enough "because social institutions and cultural ideals are rooted in patriarchy, and patriarchy is rooted in fundamental biological differences, namely, differences in muscular strength and sexual reproduction."[72] Radical Feminists see great promise in artificial wombs, some going as far as to argue for their necessity. Until women are untethered from the unfair burden of pregnancy, true equality with men is impossible.

Finally, Cultural Feminists emphasize the importance of relational ties and their resulting moral obligations. They worry that artificial wombs would make women obsolete, leading to the devaluing of mothering, and with it the devaluing of women generally, and even children.

So artificial wombs might free women from the burdens of pregnancy and empower many to have children who otherwise couldn't. It might usher in an age of sexual equality, the ultimate sexual unfairness finally rectified. But it might also undermine the social valuation of mothering and, as a result, the status of women and kids.

Sander-Staudt ultimately concludes the technology should only be pursued for medically therapeutic reasons, and not as a convenient alternative to natural pregnancy, because artificial wombs would be "inherently demeaning

---

72 "Of Machine Born?," page 115.

and disempowering to women as biological mothers."[73] However, Singer and Wells disagree.

> We, at least, are not nearly so pessimistic about the abilities of women to achieve equality with men across the broad range of human endeavors. For that reason, we think women will be helped rather than harmed by the development of a technology that makes it possible for them to have children without being pregnant.[74]

Cultural Feminists are right that were most people gestated in artificial wombs, society might forget how women were once the exclusive bearers of human life. However, the suggestion isn't that natural pregnancy should stop, but that terminal abortions could stop, replaced by artificial womb transplants.

For this limited purpose, a substantial negative impact on the social valuation of mothering seems unlikely. In fact, it might affirm the difficulty of mothering and increase social respect for it. The technology wouldn't make much difference when it's the child's expected low quality of life motivating termination. But it would help a great deal

---

[73] "Of Machine Born?," page 127. Note that Sander-Staudt distinguishes between full and partial ectogenesis. With full, UDHs develop conception through birth in a machine. With partial, conception and initial gestation happen in a human mother before transplant into a machine. Full ecto has more potential to harm women's status, while partial is more relevant to abortion ethics.

[74] "Ectogenesis," page 21.

when the pregnancy is burdening the mother or the UDH is unwanted.

However, as I've learned, there are many objections. Here are a few of the better ones, followed by some possible replies.

The Risk Objection

Machines will have a hard time replacing a human womb. One obstacle: umbilical cord blood vessels are smaller than any existing surgical tubing. Another: the mix of hormones and nutrients, time-released and precisely adjusted by the mother's body, isn't fully understood. Another: growing inside a human mother could be necessary to develop a sense of empathy and compassion, without which we'd all be sociopaths. Simply *understanding* the medical miracle of gestation is hard. Safely replicating it seems almost impossible.

However, if medical progress required immediate perfection and zero risk, we wouldn't have ointments or aspirin, let alone dialysis and C-sections. When something is worth the trouble, we manage the risks and press forward.

Perhaps whatever norms governed implementation of prototype NICU feeding tubes and breathing machines could be refined and repurposed. Perhaps we could test advances on Unborn Developing Mice and then Primates, studying their long-term physical health, emotional and social wellbeing. To proactively spur emotional development, perhaps we could make the membrane soft and sound-permeable so nurses and volunteers could caress and sing to gestating UDHs.

Focusing on solutions rather than problems is a conscious choice. And since an imperfect womb is preferable to certain death, surely this is one case where we all have reason to help figure it out rather than rationalize why we shouldn't even try.

The Finance Objection

Incubating unwanted UDHs in artificial wombs would be astronomically expensive. Further, every ecto-rescue would produce an orphan. The millions of terminal abortions carried out today could become millions of additional unwanted children. How could society ever pay for this?

The costs could be split among health insurance, parents and the state. Abortion is such a divisive issue, if a country's resources should be spent on anything, they should be spent on resolving a primary scourge on stability and civic friendship. Further, religious groups, abortion advocacy groups (on both sides) and simply citizens passionate about abortion (on both sides) might be willing to donate. I would.

Just as child support payments incentivize

responsible sex today, making biological parents partially liable for an unwanted UDH's care could do the same. Maybe there are an estimated 56 million abortions globally each year[75], including more than 600,000 in the US[76], because abortion is relatively inexpensive. A stronger incentive to prevent regretful conception—not as reactive punishment, but as proactive motivation—could decrease the number of unwanted UDHs, easing the increased burden on orphanages.

We could also better honor and support single mothers. When the father skips town and times are hard, is it any surprise powdered milk and diaper vouchers aren't enough to convince more women to embrace motherhood? Serious planned parenthood education in schools and more readily available contraceptives would help. But so too would universal preschool and nursery care allowing single moms to more easily pursue a career.

In addition to funding artificial womb research, abortion solutions advocate Kevin Degidon suggests extending safe haven laws that allow parents to turn babies over to the state without further obligation, as well as

---

75 "Fact Sheet: Induced Abortion Worldwide," Guttmacher Institute, 2018. http://www. https://www.guttmacher.org/fact-sheet/induced-abortion-worldwide

76 "In 2018, 619,591 legal induced abortions were reported to CDC from 49 reporting areas." Center for Disease Control Reproductive Health Data and Statistics, "Abortion," https://www.cdc.gov/reproductivehealth/data_stats/index.htm

streamlining adoption procedures.[77] Notice how none of these suggestions depend on glowing orb incubators. We can partially solve abortion right now.

Worst-case scenario, perhaps artificial wombs won't be a workable solution until they're affordable. New technologies, including medical technologies, almost always get cheaper over time. And so the finance objection may eventually resolve itself.

However, we shouldn't turn that over to the market and cross our fingers. Investors have an incentive to keep costs high, so nonprofit and government research funding would likely bring about an affordable artificial womb faster.

Last, minimizing unwanted UDHs in the first place seems a wise component of any comprehensive abortion solution. So let's add to the new tech wish list a cheap, reversible infertility treatment for both sexes. Fewer unwanted UDHs would decrease aggregate costs for both artificial gestation and orphan care. Scientists, do your thing.[78]

The Unnatural Objection

Technology is OK for some things, even medical things such as prosthetic limbs, hearing aids and mechanical

---

77 For more, visit AbortionSolved.org

78 Credit to John Hardwig for suggesting this cost-saving complement.

hearts. But if anything should retain its intimate, flesh-bound origins, it's child creation and care.

Enfamil may lack the antibodies of breast milk. But assuming it's nutritious enough, evidenced by millions of healthy adults who drank it, the fact that it frees women from breastfeeding and enables men to better contribute to infant care seem good enough reasons to use it. If you're OK with baby formula, you should in principle be OK with artificial wombs. Again, in principle. No one's denying that the challenge of incubating humans will dwarf the difficulties of simply replacing natural milk.

Further, no one's arguing that artificial wombs should replace natural gestation. You can entertain that possibility if you want. But the suggestion is only that artificial wombs should nurture unwanted and otherwise doomed UDHs. Think of it this way: if a baby's options were either starving or formula, we'd agree to feed them Enfamil. Similarly, if a UDH's options are either termination or an artificial womb, the choice seems clear.

The New Normal Objection

The very existence of artificial wombs might pressure women to use them. As Sander-Staudt puts it, "pregnancy could become perceived as so primitive and disgusting that it feasibly becomes a non-choice... women who desire to retain their sexual appeal as a social power might perceive little choice but to opt for an artificial pregnancy."[79] Widespread ectogenesis could lead to "the perception of pregnancy as a disfiguring disability, pregnant women as potential contaminators of [UDHs], and birth as 'barbaric.'"[80]

This is a fair point. Cochlear implants have put similar pressure on people with hearing disabilities, which many in the deaf community resent. However, the benefit of being able to cure deafness outweighs the implicit pressure felt by people who argue there's nothing to "cure" in the first place. The same for the implicit pressure Lasik surgery puts on people with thick glasses, Rogaine puts on balding men and rhinoplasty puts on those of us with imperfect noses. That an option implicitly pressures people to exercise it isn't reason enough to declare it unethical.

Further, this objection has more to do with artificial wombs replacing natural gestation than terminal abortion. Usage for one reason could widen the door for others. But given demand from infertile couples and parents of prematurely born babies, artificial wombs are coming, ready or not. As Singer and Wells put it, the gestation gap will close "almost by accident… by doctors attempting to save the lives of premature babies."[81] A possible drawback of

---

79 "Of Machine Born?," page 114.
80 "Of Machine Born?," page 125.
81 "Ectogenesis," page 10.

using them for all pregnancies isn't reason enough to reject them for the limited purpose of supplanting abortion.

The Misuse Objection

Some object to artificial wombs because the technology could be misused. For example, what if they were repurposed to grow brainless clones, genetically engineered for organ harvest? Singer and Wells took this possibility seriously, and argued against it on grounds that it would desensitize us to the value of human life.

> [O]ur attitude of care and protection to infants goes very deep. For normal adults, these feelings are an instinctive response to the appearance and behavior of a baby… For the sake of the welfare of all our children, the basic attitude of care and protection for infants is one we must not imperil. We think this sufficient reason for rejecting, at least for the foreseeable future, the proposal to grow nonsentient [pre-conscious, unfeeling] embryos beyond the point at which they would normally have become sentient.[82]

I agree that we should resist any creepy temptation to grow brainless organ donors. However, while anticipating and heading off abuses is smart, most any technology can be misused, including kitchen knives, pain pills and the

---

[82] "Ectogenesis," page 25.

Internet. That a technology with a legitimate purpose might also be used for unacceptable purposes usually isn't reason to block its creation.

Some have argued that nuclear weapons were an exception, and I think we should slow and contain the rise of artificial intelligences.[83] But usually the risk that something may be misused isn't reason to squash it.

An Imperfect Solution

The case for artificial wombs as an alternative to terminal abortion may not be a slam dunk. But the balance of reasons does seem to lean in their favor.

New challenges would emerge, and there would definitely be drawbacks. But being able to facilitate a pregnant woman's desire to end an unwanted pregnancy and simultaneously protect the value of the UDH—the central drivers behind the hereto intractable abortion debate—seems a win-win worth pursuing. As Stellan Welin, Swedish author of the first philosophical article I read on ectogenesis puts it, "If a new technology makes it possible to avoid conflicts between legitimate interests, it is our duty to

---

[83] Super Artificial Intelligences may destroy us. Or they may hasten the creation of artificial wombs and facilitate earthly immortality. Which is more likely? Check out "The Singularity: A Philosophical Analysis" by David Chalmers and decide for yourself. Or watch my summary at YouTube.com/MattDeatonPhD.

use the new technology."[84]

However, some are proactively arguing that when artificial wombs inevitably arrive, parents should still be allowed to insist that an unwanted UDH not simply be removed, but terminated.

Is this simply a pre-ecto era defense mechanism, motivated by concern that any point ceded to the other side will be mercilessly exploited? Or are there compelling reasons why we should allow parents to terminate a UDH even when healthy and viable?

---

84 "Reproductive Ectogenesis: The Third Era of Human Reproduction and Some Moral Consequences," *Science and Engineering Ethics* (2004), 10, Page 622. Thanks to grad school buddy Dustin Nelson for sharing this article back around 2007.

Chapter 12

A Right to the UDH's Death?

While some would welcome the ability to spare an unwanted UDH's life, others might prefer the finality of terminal abortion. As ethicist Rosemary Tong puts it, sometimes rather than mere *extraction,* parents who seek abortion prefer *extinction.*[85]

We're therefore confronted with an important policy question. Once artificial wombs are safe and affordable, would it be OK to ban terminal abortions? Or should parents still be allowed to insist on a UDH's death?

Early Thoughts

Bioethicists have been considering a possible "Right to the UDH's Death" for almost fifty years. Jarvis Thomson herself qualified her pre-Roe v. Wade 1970s violinist analogy like this:

> I have argued that you are not morally required to spend nine months in bed, sustaining the life of that violinist; but to say this is by no means to say that if, when you unplug yourself, there is a miracle and he survives, you then have a right to turn around and

---

85 *Feminist Approaches to Bioethics: Theoretical Reflections and Practical Application,* Westview Press, 1997, page 131.

> slit his throat. You may detach yourself even if this costs him his life; [however] you have no right to be guaranteed his death, by some other means, if unplugging yourself does not kill him.[86]

The implication for ectogenesis-era abortion: even when it might be permissible to remove a UDH, this doesn't necessarily entail permission to kill it.

Generally pro-choice ethicist Margaret Little drew a similar conclusion decades later. Describing abortion as "ending of gestational support,"[87] she defended removal for any and all reasons, but added, "Of course, if one *could* end the assistance without effecting death, then, absent extraordinary circumstances, one should."[88]

And feminist Christine Overall, reflecting on her work published in 1987, also denied the permissibility of terminating an unwanted UDH "because the woman, I thought, had no right to the death of the [UDH] if it could survive evacuation."[89]

Changes of Heart

As neonatal technologies have advanced and the prospect of artificial wombs drawn nearer, some have

---

86 "A Defense of Abortion," page 66.
87 "The Moral Permissibility of Abortion," page 152.
88 Ibid, page 151.
89 "Rethinking Abortion, Ectogenesis, and Fetal Death," *Journal of Social Philosophy*, Vol. 46, No. 1, 2015, page 129.

revised their positions. In 2015, Overall explained why she reversed her original argument.

> I now believe that respect for the woman's bodily autonomy requires that she… be entitled not to have healthcare workers remove something from her body, against her will, with the goal of keeping it alive for purposes that are not her own…[90]

Overall defends her switch by arguing that performing a nonterminal transplant when a terminal abortion is preferred goes against the mother's will. However, were abortion clinics converted into artificial womb transplant clinics, pregnant women would be free to either carry to term or agree to a nonterminal transplant. Some might be frustrated if unable to obtain a terminal abortion. But were one to choose to undergo a transplant willingly, this doesn't seem as problematic as Overall suggests.

We might liken it to a person wanting to sell a kidney in a country where organ sales are banned but donations are allowed. While they might be frustrated, no one would kidnap and force them to donate. Removing it from their body would still be their choice. Similarly, were society to ban terminal abortions but allow ectogenetic transplants, some pregnant women might still desire a terminal abortion.

---

90 Ibid, page 130.

But no one would kidnap and force them to transplant. It would still be their choice.

It's important, however, to appreciate *why* a parent might prefer terminal abortion.

The Burdens of Biological Parenthood

Overall explains that women sometimes seek abortions not because they want to stop being pregnant, but because they don't want to create a child.

> [A] woman who seeks a termination of pregnancy does not want an individual related to herself out there, being raised by someone else. She is choosing that her future child not exist at all.[91]

Overall elaborates that giving up an unwanted UDH for adoption could trigger guilt for creating and then abandoning a human life. A mother might face social pressure to find and care for her child, or imagine it and feel shame. And she might worry about the quality of foster care her child would receive.

This is strikingly similar to the argument Hardwig offered as to why fathers should be allowed to insist on an abortion. Recall how he cited lingering worries about unfulfilled obligations many would-be fathers would rather avoid. The same could haunt the mother were her UDH

---

[91] Ibid, page 131.

brought to term in an artificial womb.

When we considered them before, these burdens didn't seem weighty enough to empower fathers to insist on an abortion today, even when adding financial burdens as well. But we may have been implicitly defending the mother, unwilling to push an unwanted abortion on her, regardless of the father's wishes.

However, strain on the mother wouldn't be a concern if she had already transferred the UDH into an artificial womb. In such cases the math would be more straightforward: the burdens of biological parenthood on the dad vs. the value of the UDH. And when the mother expresses a similar desire that the UDH be terminated, we can double the weight to account for her potential worry as well.

Even with that doubling, the same reply applies: surely a child can live an acceptably good life without their biological parents. Rather than feeling guilty for abandoning the UDH, the parents could feel reassured that their offspring has a chance at a happy life, and proud for giving it to them. If the future guilt they're imagining is motivated out of a concern for the resulting child's welfare, this should more logically inspire them to set up a trust fund or recruit good adoptive parents.

Similarly, if the mother and father would prefer their viable UDH be terminated to avoid the risk of being harassed by an estranged child, the value of the UDH still seems weightier. A parent fed up with a teenager may wish they had remained childless. But this isn't reason to justify killing them.

Of course, teenagers are full persons, whereas UDHs are only potential persons. But that potential does generate some moral value, arguably enough to override unwanting parents' potential future anguish. However, maybe we should defer to the parents' wishes nevertheless on grounds that they *own* their offspring.

An Ownership Argument

Joona Rasanen makes just that argument, that parents don't have to give good reasons to terminate their UDH because they own it.[92] The mother owns her egg, the father owns his sperm. Therefore, the parents jointly own any resulting UDH. And since owning something means being able to treat it as you please, parents should be allowed to destroy viable UDHs, even if their reasons are questionable or undisclosed.

Mathison and Davis respond that thinking of UDHs as property is wrongheaded.[93] Slavery is immoral largely because it's wrong to treat autonomous persons as mere

---

92 "Ectogenesis, Abortion and a Right to the Death of the Fetus," *Bioethics*, Vol. 31, Number 4, 2017 pages 697-702.
93 "Is There a Right to the Death of the Foetus?," *Bioethics*, Vol 31, Number 4, 2017 pages 313-320.

things. And while UDHs aren't yet autonomous persons, they do usually possess the potential to become autonomous persons, which merits similar, if not equal, treatment.

Mathison and Davis also illustrate how owning a thing doesn't always entail permission to destroy it. Consider the owner of a historical building planning to replace it with a parking lot, which the community justifiably blocks. Or imagine my Mini Australian Shepherd, Rufus. I technically *own* him. But were I to ask my vet to euthanize Rufus without good medical reason, Dr. Riggin would justifiably refuse.

The point: even if it were appropriate to think of UDHs as property, this wouldn't grant parents automatic permission to have them destroyed. If anything, the concept of stewardship seems more fitting. We empower parents to care for and make good decisions on their children's behalf, but this comes with limits and can be withdrawn in cases of severe abuse or neglect.

Of course, this analogy has its limits. As we always have to remember, there are relevant differences between UDHs and children. But in the era of safe and effective artificial wombs, one difference won't be varying survivability probabilities. A 3-day-old UDH, conceived merely three days ago, will presumably have the same likelihood of growing into a full member of the moral community as a 3-day-old baby. A 3-day-old baby would have more *realized* capacities than a 3-day-old UDH. And so all else equal, killing the baby would be more morally problematic than terminating the UDH. But in both cases, being a potential person on track to become an actual person seems enough to rule out being treated as a mere piece of property.

Post-Birth Abortion?

Some have actually argued for a parental right to the death of fully birthed, healthy babies, and even adolescent children. Christine Overall cites the arguments of other ethicists to distinguish herself from this extreme view.

> [Soren Reader] says that, at least in some cases, "[M]others do indeed, and of necessity, have the moral authority to decide the fate not just of [UDHs], but also of born babies and children"… Giubilini and Minerva give two main reasons. First, "the moral status of an infant is equivalent to that of a [UDH, in that] neither is a 'person' in the sense of 'subject of a moral right to life.'" Second, "the interests of the actual people involved matter," and in particular, the mother "might suffer psychological distress from giving her child up for adoption."[94]

The argument seems to be that since birthed babies and small children aren't yet full persons, if giving up a child

94 "Rethinking Abortion, Ectogenesis, and Fetal Death," 134.

to adoption would cause the mother mental distress, she should be able to have it killed. To her credit, Overall rejects this argument due to its unacceptable consequences.

> They include the pain and suffering of the infants killed, the violation of its right not to be killed, the negative psychological outcomes for those who would have to do the killing, and the potential deleterious effects on general social attitudes toward and relationships with babies.[95]

These are good reasons to prevent parents from killing their children (if you're amazed we're even having to discuss this, so am I). However, while Overall defends the UDH after it's removed from the womb, she argues that the mother may have it killed anytime it's still inside her.

Why allow pre-extraction extinction but prohibit it post-extraction? Overall argues that removal is "a clear and decisive criterion for [the UDH's] attainment of legitimate independent moral consideration."[96]

For sure, being inside or outside the mother is a clear demarcation. But this seems similar to arguing that so long as you're still connected to the violinist, you may permissibly shoot him. Basing executioner privileges on connection seems arbitrary. It makes more sense to say that while you have no obligation to remain connected, you also

---

95 Ibid, page 134.
96 Ibid, page 134.

have no discretion over whether a violinist or a UDH or a child lives or dies.

For some, the anguish of knowing your child is living life without you may be substantial. But we don't *kill* people because their living bothers us. We want people for whom we care to flourish, not die. Absent serious quality of life concerns, it seems warped to want someone dead because we care for them so much. And since our offspring can flourish well enough without us, insisting on their termination doesn't seem legitimate.

The Child's Quality of Life Revisited

Another quality of life concern comes not from worry over how a child might get along without its biological parents, but how unwanted children are treated generally. As articulated by Hardwig:

> Whether we should require, encourage or allow a [UDH] to become a full person depends on how unwanted children fare in our culture. I think I can imagine a society in which I would feel that we should encourage women to allow their [UDHs] to develop into personhood, especially if we had a good artificial womb. But that society is not even close to the way ours is.[97]

With little direct experience, I've been skeptical that

97 Email correspondence fall, 2020, cleared with John for publication.

unwanted UDHs' lives are terrible enough to abort as an act of mercy. Perhaps in a collapsed, war-torn country where orphans who don't starve are drafted into the military or sold as slaves would qualify. But in America, surely childhood for orphans isn't hopeless enough to abort to spare them the misery.

However, as brought to my attention by ethics student Cameron Bayer, the American Academy of Child & Adolescent Psychiatry confirms that orphans' lives are often far from ideal.

> About 30% of children in foster care have severe emotional, behavioral, or developmental problems. Physical health problems are also common.[98]

There's also evidence that orphans are more vulnerable to sex trafficking. As reported by Newsweek:

> The National Center for Missing and Exploited Children (NCMEC) found that "of the more than 18,500 endangered runaways reported to NCMEC in 2016, one in six were likely victims of child sex trafficking. Of those, 86 percent were in the care of social services when they went missing.[99]

---

98 "Foster Care," No. 64, updated October, 2018. https://www.aacap.org/AACAP/Families_and_Youth/Facts_for_Families/FFF-Guide/Foster-Care-064

99 "We Have Set Up a System to Sex Traffic American Children" by Michael Dolce for *Newsweek*, Jan 12, 2018. https://www.newsweek.com/we-have-set-system-sex-traffic-american-children-779541

These facts are sobering. While the Academy of Child and Adolescent Psychiatry affirmed in the same article that most foster children with problems show "remarkable resiliency and determination to go on with their lives," we definitely have an obligation to improve foster care, and should in any case customize quality of life predictions based on a particular UDH's situation.

An orphan in rural Tennessee might have a rosier outlook than an orphan in urban New York. Or vice versa. While I'd be inclined to err on the side of giving both a chance at happiness, we can't just cross our fingers and hope for the best. We'd have to examine the facts. And to the extent our research suggests a UDH's childhood would be miserable, and to the extent they'd be unlikely to experience redeeming joy as an adult, this would indeed count in favor of a mercy termination.

Tentative Conclusions

Neither the burdens of biological parenthood, nor the idea that UDHs are their parents' disposable property, nor worries about orphans' quality of life are reason to uphold a sweeping parental right to the death of the UDH. A UDH could be diagnosed with untreatable ailments so terrible that ending its life quickly and painlessly could be merciful. The same might be true for UDHs facing such intolerable circumstances that we can imagine them preferring to not be born at all. But for a healthy UDH in many places, these hardships wouldn't seem terrible enough.

Thus, when artificial wombs become safe and affordable, in normal cases of healthy UDHs born into stable societies, and especially to the extent that we can fix the foster care system, we will have good reason to use them to gestate unwanted UDHs, independent of whether their biological parents would prefer that they die.

Implications for Partial-Birth Abortion

If you're more interested in the ethics of today than tomorrow, the artificial wombs discussion has tested your patience. However, whether parents should be allowed to insist on a viable UDH's death isn't a question we can postpone. So-called partial-birth abortions are sometimes used to terminate late-term, fully viable UDHs today. Is this practice all-things-considered morally permissible?

Given that there's little difference between a late-term UDH still inside the mother and a birthed baby, given the weaknesses in the burdens of biological parenthood, UDH as property and foster-care quality of life arguments, partial-birth abortions for non-medical, non-mercy reasons are difficult to defend. Nevertheless, some legislatures have made them legally permissible.

This seems a political overreaction designed to counter efforts by abortion opponents. One side pushes to make abortion at any stage, for any reason, legally outlawed, so the other side pushes to make abortion at any stage, for any reason, legally allowed. Neither can admit the obvious—that both extremes are heartbreakingly callous. Rationalizations ensue, mistrust grows, and we're left with the sad state of affairs this book attempts to transcend.

Overcoming the impasse and treating abortion with the seriousness and honesty it deserves will take great courage. It's safer to continue pretending pro-this or pro-that is defendable. But I'm hopeful this book will have a civilizing, enlightening effect on abortion discussions. Beginning with your own.

Chapter 13
Pro-Both

It should now be clear that the traditional pro-choice vs. pro-life paradigm is a grossly oversimplified myth. No one value, no one right, no one argument settles anything. Instead, a rich moral ecosystem awaits exploration and balance.

The principled, compassionate, informed position seems to be Pro-*Both.* However, abortion ethics is about more than choice and life. Factors any respectable view should take into account include:

I. **The Nature of the Conception**
   a. Was the sex consensual or forced? To what degree?
   b. Was conception intentional or accidental? If accidental, were precautions taken?

II. **The Mother's Interests**
   a. Her health and life
   b. Her education, career and other life plans
   c. Her very identity

III. **The UDH's Status**
   a. Never a full person, but always a potential person, possessing some (possibly substantial) value from conception

b. Increasing in value over the course of gestation, as features of personhood emerge and survival becomes more certain

IV. **The Child's Quality of Life**

a. Biological: Likely healthy or plagued by debilitating, painful disease? How likely?

b. Circumstantial: Born into a loving family in a flourishing, supportive society, or into a neglectful system in a famine-stricken, failed state?

V. **The Father's Autonomy**

a. Respect for his reasonable assumptions, his investment of emotions and time, his plans and legitimate interests

VI. **Impact on Third Parties**

a. On siblings, grandparents and other family members who've earned consideration

b. On society at large as benefactors of future benefits or victims of future harm

If you came in hoping we'd declare UDHs full persons, the facts don't support that view. But if you came in hoping we'd declare UDHs a mere clump of cells, the facts don't support that view either. Langerak's "gradualism" helps us articulate what we intuitively knew—that later-term abortions are more morally problematic.

Sometimes it's tough to imagine circumstances dire

enough to justify an abortion not because we're coldhearted, but because we truly don't know. Pregnant women glow, they nest, they caress their bellies and wait patiently until that splendid crescendo. But whether you realize it, you know someone who's miscarried, suffered a life-threatening pregnancy complication or both.

You also probably know someone who's made the difficult decision to abort. I do, and understanding their torturously bleak prospects made the abstract thought experiments far more personal. If no one's confided their story to you, the Rate That Abortion cases were inspired by real life: the 13-year-old raped by her mother's boyfriend, the woman pregnant with her just-divorced husband's child, the family on the verge of homelessness, the woman diagnosed with cervical cancer.

While judging is part of the ethicist's job, only the fool judges proudly. As retired Air Force Chaplain Len Zeller puts it, "When the decision to have or not have an abortion becomes real and personal, I have seen people make a 180-degree shift from their theoretical positions."[100]

Whatever our armchair judgments, women who seek abortions deserve our compassion and empathy. We can't possibly fully understand their circumstances, nor can any of us be sure how we would react were it our health, life,

---

[100] Email correspondence October, 2020, cleared with Len for publication.

body and identity on the line.

The interests of men are usually excluded from the discussion, and rightly so. Sex is hardly burdensome, and it's the woman who faces the health risks, the disrupted life, the permanently changed identity. But as Harris argued, raising a family really is centrally important to some men. And when a man invests himself emotionally, temporally and financially in a life partner to the exclusion of all others, it seems reasonable to expect her—absent mitigating circumstances—to honor the agreement.

However, Hardwig's point was that some men have equally strong interests in *not* procreating. A one-night stand can lead to an unwanted child, crushing guilt and wages garnished so heavily that working no longer seems worth the trouble. The desire to avoid these consequences is reason enough to use contraceptives and choose our sexual partners carefully. But is it also reason enough to justify killing a UDH?

Hardwig thought so, and so did defenders of a right to the UDH's death. You're welcome and encouraged to judge all arguments for yourself. But I found them lacking. UDHs aren't yet persons. But especially in the case of late-term pregnancy today and artificial wombs in the future, not only are they potential persons, but fully viable, and once removed from the mother, causing no substantial burden to either parent.

Artificial Wombs, Genuine Hope

Whether they arrive via a single technological breakthrough or steady progress, human incubators are coming. While I'm excited by the possibilities, others are anxious.

Some objections are motivated by unease over supplanting natural gestation. However, the limited usage of NICUs to sustain premature babies doesn't undermine the status of women or mothering today. Limited usage of artificial wombs to gestate unwanted UDHs wouldn't necessarily do it in the future, either.

It would be naïve to believe artificial wombs could never be used in nefarious ways. But just because a technology risks being hijacked for Frankensteinian purposes doesn't mean we shouldn't pursue it. Abuse can't be fully prevented. But it can be minimized. No super-soldier clone armies or Matrix-style human batteries, please.

We saw how the Unnatural Objection is overridden by the technology's lifesaving potential, similar to how we might prefer breastmilk, but accept formula. If sustaining the life of a young human in an unnatural way is permissible in one case, it would seem permissible in the other.

The Finance Objection, while powerful, can be overcome with support from biological and adoptive parents, the state, insurance companies and those most interested in resolving the abortion war, such as religious organizations, pro-choice and pro-life advocates and (fingers crossed) future Pro-Both organizations as well. To check out what may be the first, visit AbortionSolved.org. If nothing else, we may simply have to wait to solve abortion until artificial wombs are affordable.

And the Risk Objection can be mitigated by adopting artificial wombs slowly, carefully, and only when the chances of birth defect are outweighed by the hope of surviving to enjoy an acceptably happy life. Certain ethicists specialize in medical research, and more of them will apply their talents to this question soon. But the fact that Neonatal Intensive Care Units have progressed to their current state without significant backlash suggests the viability date could be ethically pushed back to conception.

Some will confuse artificial womb progress as a threat to reproductive autonomy and mobilize to defend the abortion-termination connection. Others will perceive it as an affront to the natural order and insist on full, natural gestation, regardless of the impact on mothers. In response to the "right to the UDH's death" arguments, expect counterarguments defending a proposed "right to natural gestation." And expect me to shake my head at the language of rights.

Political Predictions

Still fixated on total victory and fearing total defeat, some will attack the solution to maintain donations to a favored interest group or support from single-issue voters. Ben Sharpton suggests one way this might play out in *The 3rd Option*. If you like politically charged sci-fi, check it out.

My hope is that the reasonable majority will see the promise and demand we at least try. Surely the civic friendship and solidarity resolving the abortion debate would bring is worth the trouble. Surely it's wiser to pursue a win-win than to force a win-lose.

Disagreement over other matters would persist. But as *the* anchor issue for so many, abortion drives us to rationalize inconsistent, destructive position clusters on everything from guns to the environment, immigration to defense. As Court Lewis puts it:

> The Right claims to be pro-life, yet promotes policies that undermine healthcare, education and social support. The Left claims to be in favor of protecting society's most vulnerable, yet is pro-choice, discounting the vulnerability of UDHs.[101]

Loosening abortion's grip on politics would give us space to think. And my bet is that when people get a taste of

---

[101] Shared via commentary on this manuscript December, 2020, cleared with Court for publication.

reconciliation and principled balance, most will want more. In that way, solving abortion could save democracy.

Parting Requests

Our culture oddly demonizes intellectual growth, as if clinging to a petrified view is something to be proud of. It takes courage to admit we may have been wrong, our understanding incomplete. But my goodness, surely we can be humble enough to concede that we don't have everything figured out. If my own views are the same five years from now, I'll consider it a deep failure. Not because change is good for its own sake, but because there's always more to learn.

Revisit Rate That Abortion to see how your own view has evolved. Can you now articulate the reasoning behind what began as mere hunches? Which previously dim factors now shine bright? Which cases deserve the biggest score adjustment? Can you now better appreciate why someone might reasonably disagree?

Take a shot at some of the cases we didn't return to. In Y, parents Yasmine and Yasir are considering aborting to avoid population control sanctions. In Z, the UDH is female, but Zelda and Zack want their firstborn to be male. In AA, the UDH is male, but Arsheen and Aaron need it to be female to receive a substantial inheritance. In FF, Fabio is encouraging Florencia to abort and take that long-planned trip around the world. In HH, heroin-addicted father Hank promises to go to rehab if Hanita aborts. In II, young Isabelle and boyfriend Ignacio didn't use contraceptives because they didn't intend to go all the way. And in JJ, young Janet didn't intend to go all the way with her boyfriend, either. Yet this would be her third abortion for that reason.

Tempted to slap down a number and move on? You know better. Pushing ourselves to pursue wisdom over comfort is an ongoing battle. Maybe that Original Position thought experiment from the Third Parties chapter would help? That Rawls guy may be onto something…

Thank you for trusting me to lead you through this most difficult of issues. My ego is just as sneaky as the next person's, my tendency to rationalize just as pervasive. My only hope is that I've done these arguments enough justice to allow you to fairly judge them, and provided a rich enough framework for you to sketch your own view.

However, ethics isn't something one wise philosopher can sit back and dictate. So try to work with, rather than against, one another, and I promise to do the same.

Remember that it's a high-stakes, personal subject, that none of our positions are perfect, and that not so long ago we ourselves underestimated its complexity.

And when you hear someone using "fetus" or "baby," look them in the eye, smile and kindly offer UDH.

Even if the term doesn't stick, maybe the approach will. That is this way—the philosopher's way. Welcome.

If you enjoyed
Abortion Ethics in a Nutshell,
please tell a friend or write a
brief review.

Cheers,
& thanks so much for reading.

More Books by Matt Deaton

Ethics in a Nutshell

The Philosopher's Approach to Morality in 100 Pages (2017)

Why morality is distinct from and precedes legality, how philosophical ethics is compatible with religious moral reasoning, why ethics can't be a mere matter of personal taste, how to build and analyze moral arguments by analogy, the four dominant ethical theories—stuff any good college ethics course would cover, plus concise, accessible, laid-back.

Listen to it on audiobook in 100 minutes, or visit EthicsinaNutshell.org for mini-lectures on each chapter, editable syllabi and other resources for teachers and students alike.

Year of the Fighter
Lessons from my Midlife Crisis Adventure
(2018)

★★★★★ 46 ratings

What it felt like to step in the ring for the first time, to do it against fighters half my age, and to sometimes win. The joys of punching dudes in the face (hey, ethicists aren't supposed to say that...), of being so exhausted (and possibly concussed) that I puked, and what it took to make a lifelong dream reality.

Basically, that human autonomy stuff in action. Plus coaching for tackling *your* adventures, reflection on how life's brevity gives us all reason to act sooner rather than later and just a dash of combat art ethics.

The Best Public Speaking Book

2nd Edition (2019)

The world needs more ethically-minded speakers. So conquer stage fright with the "Urban Honey Badger" assertiveness drill. Organize your messages so they're easy to remember and deliver. Discover and polish your authentic stage self. Don't simply *survive* on stage. Decide to *dominate*.

Based on my experience going from terrified rookie to conference presenter, paid keynote speaker and comedy club host, as well as years coaching students in my oral-concentration philosophy classes. The core: *Know Thy Material, Be Thyself* and *Practice.*

Ethics Bowl to the Rescue!

How the Anti-Debate is Saving Democracy

(coming 2022)

From Los Angeles to Long Island, Washington state to Washington, D.C., Texas to Tennessee, ethics bowls are a rising counter to the caustic, childish forces destroying civic discourse. Dubbed the "anti-debate" by Michigan High School Ethics Bowl organizer Jeanine DeLay, these transformative events are saving democracy, one participant at a time.

Based on interviews with over two dozen coaches, organizers, judges and participants from as far away as Australia and China, learn why ethics bowl deserves its stellar reputation and your support.

If you're an educator considering assigning one of my books, desk copies and teaching resources are on the house.

Be on the lookout for all my titles on audiobook fall, 2021.

And to connect, visit MattDeaton.com.

www.ingramcontent.com/pod-product-compliance
Lightning Source LLC
Chambersburg PA
CBHW030329100526
44592CB00010B/622
* 9 7 8 1 9 5 1 6 7 7 0 6 0 *